Read On . . . Historical Fiction

Read On . . . Historical Fiction

Reading Lists for Every Taste

Brad Hooper

Read On Series

A Member of the Greenwood Publishing Group

Westport, Connecticut • London

Library of Congress Cataloging-in-Publication Data

Hooper, Brad.
    Read on—historical fiction : reading lists for every taste / by Brad Hooper.
        p. cm. — (Read on series)
    Includes bibliographical references and index.
    ISBN 1-59158-239-3 (pbk. : alk. paper)
    1. Fiction in libraries—United States. 2. Historical fiction, American—Bibliography.
3. Historical fiction, English—Bibliography. 4. Readers' advisory services—United
States. 5. Public libraries—United States—Book lists. I. Title. II. Series.
Z711.5.H65   2006
016.813'8109—dc22   2006003711

British Library Cataloguing in Publication Data is available.

Library of Congress Catalog Card Number: 2006003711
ISBN: 1-59158-239-3

First published in 2006

Libraries Unlimited, 88 Post Road West, Westport, CT 06881
A Member of the Greenwood Publishing Group, Inc.
www.lu.com

Printed in the United States of America

The paper used in this book complies with the
Permanent Paper Standard issued by the National
Information Standards Organization (Z39.48–1984).

10   9   8   7   6   5   4   3   2

Contents

Introduction

As young people would say these days, historical fiction "rules." True, novels set in the historical past have been around for as long as the novel form itself; the historical romances of Sir Walter Scott are prime examples of early historical novels. (I use "historical fiction" and "historical novels" interchangeably throughout this book; the other fictional form, the short story, has never seemed to be a comfortable home for treatments of the historical past.) But these days historical fiction is not simply a minor component of the fictional output, regarded as a "genre" of fiction, with all the pejorative thinking that goes into that label leveled at any body of fiction; no, today historical fiction is hot.

Writers of considerable literary talent are writing historical novels, publishers appear only too eager to add them to their lists, and readers—whether patrons of bookstores or the local public library—line up to consume them. As the book you have in your hands right this minute was being written, for example, the highly esteemed American fiction writer Philip Roth was enjoying critical praise as well as *New York Times* best-seller status for his amazing novel *The Plot Against America*, a highly imaginative and even frightening novel that poses the alternate historical proposition that famous aviator Charles Lindbergh was elected president of the United States in 1940.

The point is, historical fiction has gained a popularity and respect in recent years that is unprecedented in the history of this type of fiction. This "renaissance," if you will, can be charted back to the publication of Charles Frazier's riveting, extremely popular Civil War novel *Cold Mountain*, which appeared in 1997. Frazier's editor at Atlantic Monthly Press hit a gold mine when she acquired this first novel. And readers simply could not get enough of the richly detailed and tragic tale of love set in a historical period that is inherently brimming with political and personal drama, and which continues to draw in the consciousness and interest of readers who do not necessarily regard themselves as students of history, American or otherwise. That is, of course, one of the magical abilities of historical novels in the first place, as well as their primary "function": to take readers back into history with the benefit of accuracy of time and place but without the burden of the all-too-often dry professorial lecture from a podium. Certainly most of us with degrees in history greatly enjoy nonfiction books on historical topics and do indeed remember fondly many of our history professors, but not all of the reading public is interested in approaching history as an academic subject.

The Appeal of Historical Fiction

I am astonished at the number of historical novels that have as their chief character, or at least as a secondary character who nonetheless casts a deep shadow over the primary ones, England's great Tudor queen, Elizabeth I. At least two series of mystery novels feature Elizabeth I or at least are set at the court over which she presided. And these novels, the mysteries as well as the "straight" historical ones, prove very popular with the reading public.

Why do readers who obviously would not consider themselves particularly avid and knowledgeable followers of sixteenth-century European history so readily and comfortably sit down with a novel about Elizabeth I? The answer lies in the word *intrigue*. It is a word—*the* word, actually—most often associated in the general reader's consciousness, or most often used in reviews and publicity blurbs, with the times in which Elizabeth I lived and the environment at her court. Intrigue of courtiers jockeying for the queen's favor; intrigue of her enemies abroad (or, rather, enemies of England and its growing might); and intrigue fostered by, or at least in the name of, Elizabeth I's cousin and Catholic claimant to the English throne, Mary, Queen of Scots. Add to that the element of romance—Elizabeth I's fascination with handsome young men, most notably her two famous favorites, the Earl of Leicester and the Earl of Essex—and the perennial question that undoubtedly will never be answered: How intimate was she with them sexually?

Last but not least when it comes to defining Elizabeth I's appeal to a general reading public is her attractiveness as a strong female character, one who never compromised her position or power, even to the point of refusing to marry.

To understand, then, the appeal of Elizabeth I to a readership not otherwise drawn to sixteenth-century European history is to understand the appeal of historical fiction *in the first place:* It teaches us about history, but, as I stated previously, without the tedium of the podium, intervening between the reader and the enjoyment of history. Too many people consider history a dry, boring subject; I am afraid such a sentiment is the result of too many history *teachers* being dry and boring.

No one likes being lectured to, most especially in the field of history. But history, I insist, is truly a dynamic subject, brimming with *real* people (though actually deceased by this point, of course!), and what historical fiction does, or should do if it is worthy of the name, is serve to remove the podium standing between the reader and the reader's probable fascination with history. The inherent excitement of historical figures and events can be enjoyed by the general reading public on their own. In a good historical novel, readers can step in and *live* the historical past, and not simply—and dryly—be talked to about it by a boring history teacher.

Let us return to the reception accorded *Cold Mountain*. Another aspect of that novel's impact was that in the wake of its critical and commercial success, fiction editors at highly regarded publishing houses went on the lookout for its successor, for the next manuscript that would not only make history exciting but also *make* history; that is, bring in the kind of revenue *Cold Mountain* saw, in hardcover and paperback sales and movie rights as well. What such publisher eagerness has meant to the reading public is that, revenue surprises and surpluses aside, an increased number of excellent historical novels have enjoyed publication in the few years since *Cold Mountain*'s appearance, demonstrating an amazing range of themes, time periods, characters, and fictional method.

The rule appears to be that if readers read them, they will be published. (It bears keeping in mind that this post–*Cold Mountain* renaissance has contributed in no small part to the current commercial success of historical fiction; for the renaissance to continue, historical fiction must continue to sell, and sell well.) The reader can only stand to benefit from such a situation: keep it up ("it" being one's reading appetite for historical novels), and you will get more and more of them. What a marvelous reward. Where else in life is such a win-win situation offered?

Naturally, this proliferation of historical fiction can leave the enthusiastic reader bewildered about what to select that would be a suitable match for his or her interests and taste, as well as leaving the librarian uncertain what next to recommend to the avid historical fiction readers among their patrons. Consequently, we offer this handbook as an aid in matching readers to books—making it not only a productive activity, but also an absolutely fun one, avoiding as much as possible a hit-or-miss experience and making certain a majority of the exercises are "hits."

Definition, Types, and Criteria for Selection

First I offer my working definition of historical fiction, the fundamental "truth" upon which this book is built. A historical novel, by tradition and by my working plan, is qualified to be called that if it is set 50 years prior to the date it was written. A novel written today and taking place in village-and-country-town England in the early nineteenth century certainly fits this definition; Jane Austen's novels, set in that time and place and also *written* in those years, do *not*. In this book I focus on the former kind.

However, on some—but very infrequent—occasions I have violated that rule. A handful of novels that were written *during* the period in which they were set do appear within the pages of this book. I include them (and indicate in the annotations which ones they are) because they give such indelible impressions of the particular place and time in which they are set that readers interested in learning about the period can benefit greatly from reading these particular choices. All novels tell something about their cultural context; the few I have chosen merit inclusion here because they share their setting so well, in other words, as original documents.

Classic historical novels most definitely fall within my purview here, and they should be promoted by librarians every chance they get to place a historical novel in a library patron's hands. Classic novels should never be excluded from the repertoire of historical fiction readers out of some mistaken notion that "old" means creaky and stuffy. Standing the test of time has *much* to say for itself.

But that said, I place greater emphasis in this book on historical fiction published within the past few years. The classics are easier for librarians and readers to discover than finding good literature or good entertainment within the plethora of titles in the post–*Cold Mountain* era. That is where I—through this book—step in, as a guide—a beacon in the night—to sorting though that proliferation.

Generally, there are two kinds of historical novels. The first is accomplished by the author taking from the pages of history an actual figure—one who certifiably lived in years past—and spinning fictional scenes and dialogue to make that character so viable that contemporary readers can recognize and appreciate him or her as a real person, while at the same time answering to the responsibility of presenting the character with overall historical accuracy.

The second kind of historical novel is achieved by inventing characters to fit in an accurately rendered time and place, to reflect that particular setting and convey the general types of individuals who lived there. Frequently the writer of historical novels will choose to combine historical and fictional characters in historically accurate times. Both kinds of historical novel are included in this guide.

For the most part, the focus here is on novels that emphasize history, not romance with a historical bent or mystery in a historical setting, but rather those novels in which visits to the past are their primary, overriding raison d'être.

Organization and Intent

This is a book of lists, rather than a formal reference guide to the genre. The lists include common features of books that may not necessarily be identified elsewhere. The book is divided into five categories corresponding to the major factors by which historical novels appeal to readers: setting, story, character, language, and mood and atmosphere. Each chapter is subsequently divided into more specific categories, which cut across traditional ways of categorizing historical novels, arriving at what I hope are some intriguing and special ways of identifying and suggesting novels that will appeal to a wide range of interests.

The categories are a nontraditional, even whimsical, "shakeup" of the field of historical fiction.

I do not aim at comprehensiveness but simply offer associations between novels that most readers will not have realized before. For each of these specific categories I include five to ten recommended titles, each annotated and with the appeal identified. The appeal of a particular book varies from reader to reader. I have tried to group books within appeal categories that are common to many readers. However, assigning appeal features is not a science, and any given appeal can always be argued. Likewise, it may sometimes appear obvious why I placed a certain novel in a particular category, but in other instances the reason for my placement may be less apparent. The annotations clarify why I have chosen a particular category over other categories that might qualify. Obviously many novels could stand in a second or even third or fourth category, but I have selected the one that either most suits it or distinguishes it in a way that would not otherwise occur to potential readers of that particular title.

Format

Many historical novelists write series of interconnected novels that continue a storyline from one individual novel to the next, in a form of serialization. If the volumes in the series are perfectly capable of standing alone—that is, are completely understandable and embraceable on their own, without having to read predecessors in the series—then I have decided to treat them all separately, or have selected a few of the best in the series to annotate separately. On the other hand, I have combined volumes in a series (or at least a selection of them) into one entry and annotation if I found that they are best read not as individual, freestanding entities but rather as components of the author's larger picture.

The year cited in the entry for each title is the year of original publication, not necessarily the year of publication of the edition cited.

How to Use this Book

These bibliographies are intended for the collection development librarian, the readers' advisory librarian, the fiction-reading clientele in the public library, booksellers, and general readers looking for new reading material in the bookstore. They present many recommendations within a rich and wide range of historical fiction, from light to literary, from educational to entertaining. These are unconventional and even sometimes whimsical reading lists, meant as professional reading for readers' advisors and booksellers who wish to better acquaint themselves with the genre and its newer publications, particularly in terms of appeal factors. The readers' advisor may sometimes use it to identify read-alikes rooted in shared appeal factors or the specific characteristics on which the lists are based. Finally, the book is meant as a source for booklists that librarians might post on their Web sites, place in newsletters, or use in handouts to patrons. However the book is used in the short term, I hope it will ultimately assist readers in finding the books they enjoy.

Closing

A final word about how best to view the entire rich, exciting body of historical fiction. One of the finest practitioners in the field, Marguerite Yourcenar, author of the classic historical novel *Memoirs of Hadrian*, made this statement about the composition of her novel: "Those who put the historical novel in a category apart are forgetting that what every novelist does is only to interpret, by means of the techniques which his period affords, a certain number of past events; his memories, whether consciously or unconsciously recalled, whether personal or impersonal, are all woven of the same stuff as History itself."[1]

Notes

1. Marguerite Yourcenar, *Memoirs of Hadrian* (Pocket, 1977), 250.

Chapter 1

Setting

"Setting" is defined most succinctly as "time and place." That is, in what particular geographical location and during what time period does the novel's plot unfold? Setting is the primary factor readers use to identify a historical novel, the most prevalent factor they respond to. Setting is generally the appeal element a library patron can most readily and easily use to describe the novel he or she has just enjoyed, and now would like the librarian to help him or her find a novel just like it.

Setting is also the most common and obvious way of sorting historical fiction into categories: Civil War or medieval Europe or twentieth-century Latin America, and so on. The length of the list depends on how many subcategories the sorter/lister divides the categories into, from the most general to the almost minutely specific.

In this handbook I eschew the ordinary separations/designations by setting, offering instead a set of new, provocative, and creative arrangements. For librarians and for readers of historical fiction, finding a list of novels set in Renaissance Italy, for instance, presents no great challenge. But why not shake up the mix and link novels by more subtle and more intriguing, imaginative, and rewarding categories, with each novel placing primary emphasis on setting but the linkage being nontraditional, a new way of looking at how the author handles setting? The novels cited and annotated in this chapter share an emphasis on the use of setting; all offer distinctive past times and places. But they have been connected by categories readers may not have considered before.

Lost Worlds of Privilege

Gone with the wind are these settings that once upon a time offered their inhabitants a cosseted life.

Bassani, Giorgio.
    The Garden of the Finzi-Continis. **1962.** Harcourt. paper. 204pp. ISBN 0-15-634570-6.

        Novels often explore the effects of fascism on personal life in the 1930s in Germany, but this well-regarded Italian novelist offers a brilliant, heart-aching depiction of *Italian* Jewry on the eve of their destruction, in a novel about the private and protected world of a distinguished Ferrarese Jewish family. Their insularity is obvious, and the coming tensions cast a shadow over the whole place.

Bowen, Elizabeth.
    The Last September. **1929.** Random. paper. 320pp. ISBN 0-385-72014-9.

        Bowen was a highly regarded novelist and short-story writer descended from the Anglo-Irish Ascendancy, the Irish families of English Protestant descent who constituted the gentry in pre-independent Ireland. This, her second novel, does not technically qualify as a historical novel, not having been written at least 50 years after the time in which it is set, but because it so accurately, vividly records the state of the Anglo-Irish Ascendancy in the 1920s—as their privileged status was declining and their so-called Great Houses destroyed—it is an important historical, though fictionalized, document about Ireland during the "Troubles." It is also a carefully understood coming-of-age story about a young woman, and that has its appeal as well here, as does Bowen's trademark lush, even luxurious, writing style.

Cather, Willa.
    Sapphira and the Slave Girl. **1940.** Vintage. paper. 320pp. ISBN 0-394-71434-2.

        The last novel by this major American writer reflects her transcendent interest in the state in which she was born—Virginia—despite her long preoccupation with the Nebraska of her youth. This is antebellum Virginia, and this novel is an eloquent depiction of life and customs (and psychology) in a slave society, the plot centering on a white woman born "aristocratic" but who married beneath her, and her jealousy about her husband's interest in one of their young slave girls.

Colegate, Isabel.
The Shooting Party. **1980.** Counterpoint. paper. 208pp. ISBN 1-58242-222-8.

In the autumn of 1913, a country-house party assembles at an English aristocrat's Oxfordshire estate, at the apogee of the opulent Edwardian era: fancy clothes, elaborate meals, and wholesale slaughter of game. But soon a tragic accident brings an end to the party, just as World War I will soon precipitate the end of aristocratic privilege in Britain and across the rest of Europe.

Davis-Goff, Annabel.
The Fox's Walk. **2003.** Harvest. paper. 336pp. ISBN 0-15-603010-1.

World War I rages on the Continent, and at the same time revolutionary ferment in Ireland is spreading and intensifying. Born into a privileged Anglo-Irish family, young Alice, who narrates this novel, gathers from the adult conversations upon which she eavesdrops (she is left in the care of her deeply old-fashioned grandmother) a growing sense of the impending fall of the world she inhabits. The Great Houses of the Protestant elite will actually fall to the torch as the old order refuses to change with the times. Little Alice, with precocious sensibility and sensitivity, must face both growing up quickly and the future of her insolated society—which has no future. An interesting take on these crucial events from a child's increasingly mature perspective, and even richer when read along with Elizabeth Bowen's *Last September* (see above).

De Lafayette, Madame.
The Princess of Cleves. **1678.** New Directions. paper. 240pp. ISBN 0-811-21070-7.

In a simple, graceful style, with exquisite psychological understanding of its characters, this classic of French literature takes a delicious peek at the passions and machinations of the brilliant seventeenth-century court of Henry II of France: "never was there a court with so many beautiful ladies and handsome men." Her prose leaves the reader actually seeing them. For readers who love to be whisked away to share with royalty how they lived and spent their days, this novel cannot be topped.

Ishiguro, Kazuo.
The Remains of the Day. **1989.** Vintage. paper. 245pp. ISBN 0-394-25134-2.

The critically well-regarded Ishiguro, who also enjoys a large following among the discriminating general fiction reading public, is the author of a deeply layered——but certainly not labored—novel that was made into a successful movie in 1993. (The novel won the prestigious Booker Prize in Great Britain.) With a subtle, understated prose style, Ishiguro penetrates deeply into both one man's psychology and the English social order he is part of. In the late 1950s, an elderly butler, who has carefully, snobbishly, and even blindly served his master, Lord Darlington, for 30 years, takes a physical trip—a drive by himself across the English countryside—and a metaphorical trip as well, down memory lane. The emptiness of complete devotion to others as a personal way of life and as part of a social system dawns on him as his journey unfolds.

Márai, Sándor.
   Embers. **1942.** Vintage. paper. 213pp. ISBN 0-375-40756-1.
   From a leading twentieth-century Hungarian novelist (who died in 1989) comes a beautifully articulated and deeply imagined (psychologically) novel about friendship, betrayal, and revenge, set in a remote Hungarian castle early in World War II. The mores and codes of the Austro-Hungarian Empire are the backdrop to a dialogue-driven narrative featuring an old general who came of age in the glory days of the Hapsburg Empire and is now bent on settling a long-unresolved score with the man who was his best friend. Those old codes of empire were extremely stiff, but this novel is quite supple.

Scott, Paul.
   The Jewel in the Crown. **1966.** University of South Carolina. paper. 462pp. ISBN 0-226-74340-3.
   The Day of the Scorpion. **1968.** University of South Carolina. paper. 483pp. ISBN 0-226-74341-1.
   The Towers of Silence. **1972.** University of South Carolina. paper. 400pp. ISBN 0-226-74343-8.
   A Division of the Spoils. **1975.** University of South Carolina. paper. 597pp. ISBN 0-226-74344-6.
   These four interconnected novels comprise the Raj Quartet, a highly detailed, character-packed, and, as readers have found with each novel's publication, deeply absorbing depiction of the last years of British rule in India (from the late 1930s to the late 1940s). The most interesting aspect of these novels (which are complete unto themselves but are most effective when read together, to see a complete tapestry of characters and events) is the revelation of class conflict within the British ruling class, a pecking order within the pecking order.

Settle, Mary Lee.
   Know Nothing. **1960.** University of South Carolina. paper. 340pp. ISBN 1-57003-116-9.
   Settle brings the story of the Virginia families introduced in the previous volume in her celebrated Beulah Quintet, *O Beulah Land*, up to 1821 to 1861. A plantation master, owner of slaves, sees two sons enlist on opposite sides when the Civil War breaks out. In this installment in particular, Settle is heavily concerned with social customs and observing the families she has been limning from one generation to another as they move up the social ladder. The novels in this riveting quintet are so rich they actually should be read separately, not necessarily in order, nor one immediately after the other.

Welty, Eudora.
Delta Wedding. **1945.** Harvest. paper. 336pp. ISBN 0-15-625280-5.

The best novel by a greatly beloved American fiction writer explores, within the culture of her native Mississippi, the social mores of a family of privilege in the early 1920s. Technically this novel does not qualify as historical fiction (it is not set at least 50 years prior to when it was written). Its inclusion here is warranted by the picture Welty so knowingly and vibrantly paints, as an extended family gathers on a Delta plantation for a wedding, of both the subtleties of family dynamics (the allusions and alliances made between family members and the nuances of their social decline) and a moment of white power frozen in time, which, within the family context depicted here, is sensitively exerted but nevertheless represents an unbalanced equation between the races. The system of legalized inequality of opportunities is not as pronounced as it was in the days of, say, *Gone with the Wind*, but nevertheless, behind the nice clothes and nice cars, there is still the shadow, second-class world of blacks.

Old New York

Take a stroll down Fifth Avenue when high society ruled in New York City.

Ephron, Amy.
A Cup of Tea. **1998.** Ballantine. paper. 200pp. ISBN 0-345-42570-7.

Based on a short story of the same title by the great New Zealand writer Katherine Mansfield, this tragic, tightly composed (but not the least bit slight) novel takes the reader to New York in 1917. A love triangle among a couple of considerable means and the young woman of no means whom the pampered woman, out of charity, brings into their home sets in motion a chain of events that changes these three lives forever. One can hear the rattle of oh-so-proper teacups.

Ephron, Amy.
One Sunday Morning. **2005.** Morrow. 214pp. ISBN 0-06-058552-8.

The author of *A Cup of Tea* and *White Rose* offers a precise and concise yet deeply spirited novel of manners set in the New York and Paris of the 1920s. Four women friends seek love and have a brush with mysterious death and consequent social scandal. This is Edith Wharton territory (see below), but rendered more economically, more in keeping with contemporary stylistic tastes. The interwar years are viewed through a special prism, and illicit booze makes an appearance here as well.

Gaffney, Elizabeth.
> *Metropolis*. **2005.** Random. 416pp. ISBN 1-4000-6150-14.
>
> > Old New York offers many layers of setting for historical novels and an irresistible one for fans of the genre. This author's take on the milieu involves the growing number of gangs and immigrants in the post–Civil War city. Gaffney offers a large cast and intricate plotting as she evokes the technology, tastes, and pace of a metropolis that defines "busy" today and was obviously turbulent even then. A "New York minute" had meaning even in those days.

Wharton, Edith.
> *The Age of Innocence*. **1920.** Barnes & Noble. paper. 324pp. ISBN 1-59308-074-3.
>
> > This classic novel by one of America's most highly regarded writers reflects the milieu in which she grew up: the New York City of high society, governed by a strict code of proper behavior. Set in the 1870s, the plot deals with a young man who is engaged but falls in love with his fiancée's cousin, who was married to a Polish count but is now considering a divorce—to the consternation of proper society. (This was back when living uptown close to Central Park was considered being far away from things.)

A Slice of Americana

Through these vibrant depictions, dip into the rich tapestry of American culture at various points in its history.

Baker, Kevin.
> *Dreamland*. **1999.** HarperCollins. 512pp. ISBN 0-06-099580-7; Perennial. paper. 352pp. ISBN 0-06-093121-3.
>
> > New York City—the city of immigrants—in the early twentieth century comes electrically to life in this mixture of tales about both historical and fictitious figures. Baker uses each type to represent a portion of the patchwork of various lifestyles, locales, and events, both public and personal, that comprise the complex existence of New Yorkers, from a garment workers' strike and a gangland murder to a fire at Coney Island's Dreamland amusement park and aspects of corrupt Tammany Hall politics, the criminal underworld, and Jewish immigrant life.

Cooney, Ellen.
> *Gun Ball Hill*. **2004.** University Press of New England. 272pp. ISBN 1-58465-356-6.
>
> > As exciting as they are, the years and events leading up to the Revolutionary War—the latter including the Boston Tea Party and Paul Revere's

ride—take a back seat to how these momentous events affect ordinary lives, in this novel set in a Maine village. A family in the village is murdered by the Tories, galvanizing resistance to British rule and increasing revolutionary activity, which seems even more intense given the specific local focus.

Doctorow, E. L.
Ragtime. **1975.** Plume. paper. 270pp. ISBN 0-452-27907-0.

By one of America's most distinguished contemporary fiction writers, winner of several awards, this novel has become a contemporary classic, showing how historical figures can be effectively integrated into a true-to-life but truly lively fictional narrative. The time period covered is the twentieth century to World War I, and Scott Joplin's favorite musical style, after which is the title of the novel, also lends its syncopation to Doctorow's prose style. He captures the fabric of American life, as the country is about to assume its giant-in-the-world international status, with both accuracy and flair.

Mallon, Thomas.
Bandbox. **2004.** Pantheon. 320pp. ISBN 0-375-42116-5; Harvest. paper. 320pp. ISBN 0-15-602997-9.

The title of this novel refers to a ragingly successful magazine covering cultural issues important in 1920s New York. Crises among the staff take on paradigmatic importance as Mallon uses the magazine—in a rousingly entertaining manner—to explore the tenor of the Jazz Age: free, easy, and living life for today.

Richter, Conrad.
Sea of Grass. **1936.** Ohio University. paper. 149pp. ISBN 0-8214-1026-1.

In addition to the novels comprising the trilogy collectively called The Awakening Land, Richter also wrote this lovely but at the same time tight and sinewy novel, also set in the American West, which imparts a resonant picture of the struggle between cattlemen and farmers laying claim to and using the vast lands of the wide-open West.

Updike, John.
Memoirs of the Ford Administration. **1992.** Ballantine/Fawcett. paper. 384pp. ISBN 0-449-91211-6.

A professor at a New Hampshire junior college prepares a paper on the Ford administration that becomes a catalyst for remembering important issues in his own life during that period, including the collapse of his marriage and an ill-fated affair, and how he gave up on his attempt to write a biography of fifteenth president James Buchanan. Past and present commingle smoothly as Buchanan's and the professor's lives exhibit interesting parallels and contrasts in social history between the mid-nineteenth and the mid-twentieth centuries.

Vidal, Gore.
1876. **1976.** Vintage. paper. 384pp. ISBN 0-375-70872-3.

This intelligent and compelling novel's title was the year of the U.S. centennial, as well as the year of a disputed presidential election (along the same popular-versus-electoral-vote lines as the 2000 election). The focal point of Vidal's deeply thought-out depiction of American cultural and political processes (much of the latter corrupt) is journalist Charlie Schuyler, a character Vidal borrowed from his previous novel, *Burr.* Charlie has returned to the United States after living abroad for 35 years, and his first view of New York from the boat is of "the opulence, the grandeur, the vulgarity, the poverty, the elegance, [and] the awful crowded abundance."

White, Edmund.
Fanny. **2003.** Harper/Ecco. 384pp. ISBN 0-06-000484-3; Harper/Ecco. paper. ISBN 0-06-000485-1.

With humor and characteristic literary aplomb, White re-creates the lives of two Englishwomen who influenced opinion about American society and politics in the early- to mid-nineteenth century. Frances Trollope was the mother of novelist Anthony Trollope and wrote a negative appraisal of American life; her friend, feminist Fanny Wright, supported the abolition of slavery. The premise of White's novel is that it is a biography of Fanny Wright written by Frances Trollope, but this "biography" actually becomes Trollope's own memoirs. Two wonderfully drawn characters, but the primary draw is the novel's depiction of American life and manners in the mid-nineteenth century.

Frontier Life

Ever westward pushed the pioneers, settling the vast ocean of plain and prairie that is the North American continent.

Bittner, Rosanne.
Into the Prairie. **2004.** Forge. 250pp. ISBN 0-765-30980-7.

Falling into the "history-lite" category, this novel emphasizes fast reading over every other factor and quality. That said, the author's depiction of the settling of the West—which in the era in which this story takes place is the Ohio Valley—responsibly vivifies the hardships of frontier life, particularly the struggle between white settlers and Native Americans.

Cather, Willa.

Death Comes for the Archbishop. **1927**. Vintage. paper. 304pp. ISBN 0-679-72889-9.

In a series of heart-warming episodes, like a cycle of interconnected short stories and amounting to an exquisitely polychromatic panorama, this giant figure in American literature fashions carefully and deeply textured pictures of the land and culture of the nineteenth-century American Southwest, in the form of a fictional biography of the quietly heroic Bishop Lamy of New Mexico. The colors that play off the distant mountains, the natural aridity of the terrain, and the overarching sense of being outdoors are all beautifully caught in Cather's precise, vibrant prose. This is one of the best historical novels ever written; no one can honestly claim to be a fan of the genre without having read this exquisite yet potent novel.

Cooper, James Fenimore.

The Deerslayer. **1841**. Bantam. paper. 512pp. ISBN 0-553-21085.

The Last of the Mohicans. **1826**. Bantam. paper. 400pp. ISBN 0-553-21329-6.

These two of the best and best-loved novels in Cooper's enduring Leatherstalking Tales are rousing entertainment but also thoughtful renditions of the themes of materialism versus the mores of the frontier and the customs of white people pitted against those of Native Americans. *Last of the Mohicans* is set during the French and Indian War in colonial America, and *The Deerslayer* is set almost two decades prior. These were certainly rustic times on what was then the frontier, and extremely tense times, too, with various Indian tribes on the warpath and safety for white settlers provided only by the series of forts the Europeans built.

Fisher, Karen.

A Sudden Country. **2005**. Random. 362pp. ISBN 1-4000-6322-1.

In alternating point-of-view format, this first novel draws the reader, with the poise and verve of its prose and great historical "presence" through authentic detail, into the days when the Oregon Trail (in the 1840s) funneled settlers westward from the Eastern and Midwestern parts of the country, into a land of promise and a magnificent, awe-inspiring landscape. Lucy Mitchell is a reluctant immigrant to the West, and she insists that her husband hire frontiersman James MacLaren to guide their wagon train. Lucy and James find common emotional ground, and the novel thus gains a soulful center amid the splendor and omnipotence of the story.

Guthrie, A. B.

The Big Sky. **1947**. Bantam. paper. 400pp. ISBN 0-553-20363-0.

Fast-paced action is well matched with colorful description in this homage to the great open spaces of the American West in the early years of the nineteenth century. The story of mountain man Boone Caudill is the story of white and Indian cooperation and contests, the hunting and trapping life, and exploring the wild and natural West.

McMurtry, Larry.
Streets of Laredo. **1993.** Pocket. paper. 547pp. ISBN 0-671-53746-6.

This sequel to McMurtry's immensely popular and Pulitzer Prize–winning *Lonesome Dove* will forever dwell in the shadow of its big brother and predecessor, but nevertheless, despite its length, or even because of it, it is an atmospheric and consistently compelling narrative brimming with characters drawn deeper than the usual Old West stereotypes. Readers remember this novel for its detailed and colorful evocation of the lost world of frontier life. Dusty and dangerous, but we love to visit there via McMurtry's electric prose.

Raymond, Jonathan.
The Half-Life. **2004.** Bloomsbury. 368pp. ISBN 1-58234-448-5.

This intriguing first novel casts the present against the past as the author explores two friendships a century-and-a-half apart in time: one in early-nineteenth-century Oregon between a young male cook for a crude party of frontiersmen and a young man escaping from a group of murderous Russians; and the other, in Oregon in the 1980s, between two teenage girls living unhappily in a commune. Parallels between the two friendships are arrestingly drawn amid lush description of the ever-green Northwest.

Richter, Conrad.
The Awakening Land trilogy.

The Trees. **1940.** Ohio University. paper. 167pp. ISBN 0-8214-0978-6.
The Fields. **1946.** Ohio University. paper. 161pp. ISBN 0-8214-0979-4.
The Town. **1950.** Ohio University. paper. 300pp. ISBN 0-8214-0980-8.

This trilogy, which eventually came to be called The Awakening Land, is a superb, rich source for a fictional history of the American frontier (the rough and tumble Ohio Valley), from wilderness to the advent of industrialization, as reflected in the fortunes of a single family. The titles of the individual novels reflect the changes that occur in the process of "civilization": from rich, verdant forests to fertile fields of grain to smokestacks.

Rölvaag, O. E.
Giants in the Earth. **1924–1925.** Perennial. paper. 560pp. ISBN 0-06-093193-0.

This classic novel of frontier life, set in the Dakotas in the late nineteenth century, has a weighty thematic underpinning: how men and women can bring relevant experiences from another country into a new land and, carrying on the transposed strength to control or at least contain the earth, build a *new* country. This novel *is* the story of America, plain and simple. The smell

of plowed earth, the frigid air of the winter weather, and the breath of fresh-
ness when spring comes are sensations readily evoked by this author's
fiction.

Wescott, Glenway.
The Grandmothers: A Family Portrait. **1927.** University of Wisconsin. 412pp.
ISBN 0-299-15020-8.

Wescott was a very sophisticated member of the American expatriate
community in Paris between the world wars. Born in Wisconsin, he never
forgot his less-than-glamorous roots, and that consciousness came to fruition
in this novel, set in his native state in the nineteenth century. As the title and
subtitle indicate, it adheres to basic facts about his own life and family.
Young Alwyn Tower departs from the Midwest to taste Europe, but the
"ghosts" of his immediate ancestors, who were pioneers, accompany him on
his travels—his "flight." His acquaintance with these forebears came to
him via family photo albums and stories narrated by his grandmothers.
These pioneers—who had to wrench a living from the soil and endure extremely cold winters—had no special nobility that set them apart; the poignancy of the novel, its meaning, is that Tower's family heritage is
essentially like everyone's, a fact he recognizes, accepts, finds solace in, and
even derives self-identity from.

The Classical World

Although they flourished so long ago, ancient Greece and Rome, as well as
pharaonic Egypt and the Carthaginian empire, spring to life in the hands of good
historical novelists.

Flaubert, Gustav.
Salammbô. **1862.** Penguin. paper. 288pp. ISBN 0-14-044328-2.

The rigorous, heartbreaking psychological study *Madame Bovary* is
Flaubert's greatest masterpiece, but *Salammbô* is one of the greatest historical novels ever written. With the same painstaking realism and attention to
precise language with which he wrought *Bovary* and brought it to such brilliant literary heights, Flaubert created this total immersion in the ancient
city-state of Carthage during its heyday in the third century B.C. One vivid,
unforgettable scene follows another; the one in which lions are crucified is
both appalling and haunting.

George, Margaret.
The Memoirs of Cleopatra. **1997.** St. Martin's/Griffin. paper. 976pp. ISBN 0-312-18745-9.

> This massive yet nimble fictional biography of the (in)famous Egyptian queen takes the form of a memoir, in which Cleopatra reveals herself as more than the femme fatale: a ruler with political genius. Along the way, readers are treated to an extraordinarily rich and graphic excursion into not only the politics of the age but also all sights and smells of her world; can anyone argue that life was nothing short of precarious back then, for queen and commoner alike?

Gilchrist, Ellen.
Anabasis. **1994.** University Press of Mississippi. paper. 297pp. ISBN 0-87805-821-4.

> A favorite among the general reading public, Gilchrist here departs from her usual stage—the contemporary American South—to inhabit, with historically accurate and page-turning results, ancient Greece. This coming-of-age tale features the adolescent Auria, who flees the bonds of slavery with her mistress's cast-out baby girl. Raising the baby first on her own and eventually with the young man she marries, she constructs a life of domestic contentment amid the political crises that mark classical Greece's decline from its Golden Age to darker days. An engrossing perspective on classical Greek culture.

Pressfield, Steven.
Gates of Fire: An Epic Novel of the Battle of Thermopylae. **1998.** Doubleday. 400pp. ISBN 0-385-49251-0; Bantam. paper. 480pp. ISBN 0-553-58053-1.

> The subtitle pretty much says it all. This novel is about the battle in 480 B.C. at a mountain pass in Greece called Thermopylae, between 300 valiant but ultimately vanquished Spartan soldiers and a vast horde of invading Persian forces. Told by the battle's single survivor, this vivid narrative submerges the reader in the customs of life in the great city-state of Sparta preceding that epic struggle on the battlefield. Not exactly a gentle place in which to grow up.

Renault, Mary.
The King Must Die. **1958.** Vintage. paper. 338pp. ISBN 0-394-75104-3.
The Bull from the Sea. **1962.** Vintage. paper. 352pp. ISBN 0-375-72680-2.

> The preeminent writer of novels set in ancient Greece (see also *The Persian Boy*, probably her most famous work), Renault reveals her extensive understanding of Hellenic civilization in these two companion novels, which together tell the exciting tale of Theseus, king of Athens. The first book captures him in full force during his adventures on Crete, which included slaying the Minotaur; the second novel delves into Theseus's love for Hippolyta, queen of the Amazons. Although Renault's prose style strikes many readers

as purplish, there is no more authentic way to visit ancient Greek culture than through these novels.

At Sea

As we will see, *at sea* can mean literally on the waves or also psychologically not certain of how things lie in one's surroundings or personal life.

Keneally, Thomas.
A Victim of the Aurora. **1977.** Harvest. paper. 232pp. ISBN 0-15-600733-9.

Nonfiction books on polar expeditions abound, but this Australian writer's fictionalized version of an ill-fated expedition to the South Pole in 1909, led by Sir Eugene Stewart, brings a vividness to the privation endured like no *real* account can achieve. Sexual, racial, and class consciousness come to the fore as psychology plays a significant role in how men battle the elements to the death.

Nordhoff, Charles, and James Norman Hall.
Mutiny on the **Bounty. 1932.** Back Bay. paper. 400pp. ISBN 0-316-61168-9.

The finest example of fiction's ability to capture adventure on the high seas, this riveting and now classic novel is based on a historical incident: the voyage of the H.M.S. *Bounty* from England to Tahiti and the mutiny against the cruel Captain Bligh, led by Fletcher Christian. Flogging, lack of food and water, the unrelenting sun, and exotic beaches all contribute palpable atmosphere to this timeless and ever-exciting story.

O'Brian, Patrick.
Master and Commander. **1970.** Norton. paper. 413pp. ISBN 0-393-30705-0.

When O'Brian died in 2000 at age 85, he left behind an impressive literary legacy: his famous 20-volume cycle of high-seas adventures, the Aubrey/Maturin series. *Master and Commander* is the first and perhaps most famous volume in the series, introducing Captain Jack Aubrey of the Royal Navy and his friend, ship's doctor Stephen Maturin. Set against the backdrop of the Napoleonic Wars, this novel and its successors in the series are an amazingly compelling lesson in life aboard a man-of-war. Readers come away from these ripping good yarns familiar with the names of the various kinds of sails!

Porter, Katherine Anne.
Ship of Fools. **1962.** Back Bay. paper. 512pp. ISBN 0-316-71390-2.

The only novel by one of the most distinguished fiction writers in the history of American literature (her reputation is based on her magnificently perceived and presented short stories) took 20 years to complete. It is an engrossing read, with a huge cast of characters (therein lies many critics' problem with the novel; they found the too-numerous characters not sufficiently developed). The "ship of fools" is an ocean liner voyaging from Mexico to Germany in 1934, and life on board ship for many days is graphically depicted. But more than that, the tense political atmospheres and prejudices of that interwar period are distilled, the voyage becoming an allegory of the inherent need for humans to fall into social structures and a pecking order.

Smith, Wilbur.
Birds of Prey. **1997.** St. Martin's. paper. 664pp. ISBN 0-312-96381-5.

Perennial best seller Smith shows his stuff in this swashbuckling adventure yarn set on the high seas in the late 1600s, during a conflict between England and Holland. Sir Francis Courtenay and his teenage son, Hal, command a privateer crew that raids a Dutch ship along the African coast. Sir Francis is executed, catapulting Hal to the position of ship commander. The story is continued in *Monsoon* (see below).

Smith, Wilbur.
Monsoon. **1999.** St. Martin's. paper. 822pp. ISBN 0-312-97154-0.

This sequel to *Birds of Prey* (see above) continues the swashbuckling exploits of Hal Courtenay, a sea captain with the East India Company who, accompanied by his sons, intends to protect company ships from piracy. Set on the high seas and in Africa and Asia, battle scenes are riveting and authentic, and the drama compels quick page turning. Smith is so good at depicting his setting that the reader may even experience some motion sickness—empathetically, of course.

Small Town and Village Life

Is life slower and more relaxed outside big cities?

Byatt, A. S.
Still Life. **1995.** Scribner. paper. 400pp. ISBN 0-684-83503-7.

Byatt takes up the story of the three schoolmaster's children introduced in *The Virgin in the Garden* (see below), which was the first entry in a quartet of novels. This novel is the second installment. The focus here is on the daughter, Frederica, who is off to Cambridge, and her siblings' struggle for place and identity in the world. Not for easy reading, Byatt is quite intellectual, her novels elaborate in structure and style. Still, English life outside the great metropolis of London is richly painted: hardly a place lacking in sophistication in Byatt's hands, but without the big city's hustle and bustle.

Byatt, A.S.
The Virgin in the Garden. **1979.** Vintage. paper. 432pp. ISBN 0-679-73829-0.

Byatt, an extremely intelligent writer, has built a sturdy reputation for her marvelously perceptive and immaculately drawn novels. *The Virgin in the Garden*, her third novel, inaugurated what has become a quartet of novels (including the above mentioned *Still Life* and also *Babel Tower* and *A Whistling Woman*). This novel explores the lives of a group of individuals during the first two years (1952–1953) of the reign of the current English sovereign, Elizabeth II. Set in Yorkshire, primarily in a public school, the plot sorts through the formative, personal experiences of the three children of a master at the school, with the festive atmosphere generated by the Coronation permeating local society all the while.

Carter, Jimmy.
The Hornet's Nest. **2003.** Simon & Schuster. 480pp. ISBN 0-7432-5542-9; Simon & Schuster. paper. 480pp. ISBN 0-7432-5544-0.

Prose style and depth of characterization are not the strong points in this first novel by the former U.S. president; of course, the immediate calling card is his name recognition. Carter focuses this fictional narrative about the Revolutionary War on a generally unmined aspect of that rich vein for fiction and nonfiction writers alike: the battles that took place in the Deep South—specifically, Florida, Georgia, and the Carolinas.. His historical knowledge is impeccable, and he does best in his emphasis on local people swept up in the tide of rebellion. Simply getting food on the table, while vital to keeping body and soul together, pales in comparison to struggling for the freedom of one's country.

De Bernières, Louis.
Corelli's Mandolin. **1994.** Vintage. paper. 448pp. ISBN 0-679-76397-X.

On a Greek island where time has, if not stood still, at least slowed to glacial pace, the present in its ugliest form slaps the islanders in the face when, as World War II rages, an Italian army occupies the island. A beautiful young woman, a native of the island, is pursued by two men: a local fisherman who becomes a guerrilla fighter, and a captain in the occupation force. Dark humor mixes well with abject horror as the author testifies to the lasting effects of terror and betrayal, and goodness over evil, on this tightly knit, remote community.

Karnezis, Panos.
The Maze. **2004.** Farrar. 376pp. ISBN 0-374-20480-2; Picador. paper. ISBN 0-312-42383-7.

This first novel by a Greek-born writer living in Britain and writing in English exposes American readers to a historical episode about which most will know little: the Greek campaign into Asia Minor in the early 1920s and the Greek force's defeat by the Turks. As the Greek army retreats, one brigade has lost its bearings and wanders over the inhospitable countryside, bringing chaos to an isolated and heretofore peaceful Greek town in Asia Minor. With a large cast of colorful characters, and in lyrical language, the author offers a paradigm of war and human nature in the raw, as experienced in small, out-of-the-way places.

O'Brien, Kate.
  Without My Cloak. **1931.** Vintage. paper. 200pp. ISBN 0-86068-760-0.

In sensitively honed prose, this first novel by one of Ireland's most beloved writers delves into family life in the Irish provinces from the late eighteenth century to the latter half of the nineteenth. The supports of and the constraints upon individual will exerted by religion (in this case, Catholicism), society in general, and maintaining the good family name are carefully and absorbingly articulated. Through three generations, the Considine family climbs to the upper middle class, and upon each member is impressed the fact that Considine family loyalty is paramount, regardless of personal needs.

Rutherfurd, Edward.
  The Forest. **2000.** Ballantine. paper. 784pp. ISBN 0-345-47936-X.

Rutherford specializes in big, sprawling novels that limn the history of particular areas of England over the course of several generations. This entry in the cycle sets its sights on the New Forest, a large, wooded region in southern England. True to his custom, the author invents a small number of families of different types and presents them as paradigmatic of the evolving or devolving patterns of not only the families but also, on a grander scale, England itself.

Tripp, Dawn Clifton.
  Moon Tide. **2003.** Random. 304pp. ISBN 0-375-50844-9; paper, 320pp. ISBN 0-375-76116-0.

Into her first novel, written with lovely prose, Tripp plaits the lives of three women in a small fishing village on the Massachusetts coast, from 1913 to the Great New England Hurricane of 1938. In the process, the author explores universal truths about love, loss, sexuality, and the compulsion to violence, and how all of human nature is grounded in nature; in other words, this community is a microcosm of life, as reflected in the compelling stories of these three outwardly ordinary individuals.

Hard Times

Tales of a people beset by poverty, siege by foreign armies, oppression by outside cultural conditions, and even tyranny from foreign governments don't always feature noble individuals, but always make compelling reading.

Donoghue, Emma.
Slammerkin. **2001.** Harcourt. 352pp. ISBN 0-15-100672-5; Harvest. paper. 408pp. ISBN 0-15-600747-9.

> This novel is based on a true episode. In late eighteenth-century London, a young servant woman, born into poor, lonely circumstances and reduced to prostitution, murders the middle-class woman in whose household she is employed, driven by a craven desire to improve her station—represented in her mind by fine clothes, which, if she could come to own them, would mark her social ascent.

Foden, Giles.
Ladysmith. **2001.** Vintage. paper. 304pp. ISBN 0-375-70837-5.

> This swirling, stirring story set during the Boer War in South Africa in the last year of the nineteenth century tells the horrors of war from several perspectives. The title refers to a British outpost, which at the time the novel takes place is under siege by enemy Boer forces. Survival is more than difficult for the town's inhabitants, and this novel is good at showing the psychology of people trapped in horrific, life-and-death conditions.

Moore, Brian.
Black Robe. **1985.** Plume. paper. 256pp. ISBN 0-452-27865-1.

> Moore, Irish born but generally regarded as a Canadian writer, employed his trademark felicitous writing style on this occasion to compose a riveting, remarkably cogent portrayal of the encroachment of Jesuits in the seventeenth century into the native realms and lives of those in what is now eastern Canada. Moore understands and graphically depicts the resultant clash of cultures.

Steinbeck, John.
The Grapes of Wrath. **1939.** Penguin. paper. 455pp. ISBN 0-14-2000-66-3.

> Not a historical novel by strict definition—that is, not set at least 50 years prior to when it was written—this giant of American literature was written relatively concurrently with the time period it covers, but its powerful depiction of the economic depression of the Heartland during the Great Depression serves as an extremely effective visit—in very personal terms— to these difficult times that continue to inform our national consciousness.

The story of the Joad family and their trek to the West Coast from dust-laden Oklahoma is one that every literate American should have read by now.

Turbulence and Change

Political turbulence often leads to social change, and vice versa, and it always leads to riveting fiction.

Alvarez, Julia.
In the Time of the Butterflies. **1994.** Plume. paper. 352pp. ISBN 0-452-27442-7.
Alvarez's gripping novel is set in her native Dominican Republic and is based on the real-life Mirabel sisters (*Las Mariposas*, the butterflies, as they were called), who lost their lives in the resistance movement against the dictatorship of Rafael Trujillo. This is a very effective story of political resistance, to be read, for additional appreciation of the movement against Trujillo and a broadening of one's awareness of what was at stake in removing the dictator from office, beside Mario Vargas Llosa's magnificent novel about him, *The Feast of the Goat.*

Baker, Kevin.
Paradise Alley. **2002.** Perennial. paper. 688pp. ISBN 0-06-095521-X.
As the Civil War rages, rumors spread through the slums of New York City that a military draft is likely; of course, anyone with money would be able to buy his way out of it. Riots ensue, a horrible flair-up causing considerable damage. Baker takes this historical event and gives it a human dimension for contemporary readers by focusing on the effects of the riot on three fictional women, each a paradigm, as it were, of urban life led on a brutal edge.

Crace, Jim.
Gift of Stones. **1989.** Ecco. paper. 184pp. ISBN 0-88001-450-4.
This prize-winning British writer presents a beguiling, highly imaginative novel set just prior to the Age of Bronze in prehistoric times. In a village that retains only the knowledge and traditions of the Stone Age, villagers must confront vast changes with the advent of bronze. Highly pertinent to contemporary urban life, in which the computer has both revolutionized life and made certain tasks and workers obsolete.

Dickens, Charles.
A Tale of Two Cities. **1859.** Signet. paper. 371pp. ISBN 0-451-52656-2.
The favorite writer of many fiction lovers, Dickens began this novel about the French Revolution with one of the most famous opening lines in literature: "It was the best of times, it was the worst of times." The author brings

this absolutely momentous event down to a very personal level as these watershed times—one of the most momentous events in Western history—affect the lives of a wide cast of characters. On the other hand, he makes certain the reader never loses sight of the forest: the great social and political upheaval that was the Revolution.

Michael, Prince of Greece.
The White Night of St. Petersburg. **2004.** Grove. 352pp. ISBN 0-87113-922-7.

The author, of royal birth himself, uses his insider status and his sympathy toward and empathy for European royalty to reconstruct in fictional form the life his great uncle, who was a major force in the Romanov family in their declining years—the pre-Revolution years—of the empire. Those were days of political and familial discord and disruption, all of which are caught in high drama in this compelling novel.

Murkoff, Bruce.
Waterborne. **2004.** Knopf. 416pp. ISBN 1-4000-4038-8; Vintage. paper. 416pp. ISBN 1-4000-3258-X.

Building the Boulder Dam is both the focus and the overriding metaphor —the conquest of nature at a time of great national upset and with the sense of things being out of control—upon which this first novel rests. It is the Great Depression, and the author brings to the dam construction site, as if drawing medieval pilgrims to a holy site seeking redemption or alternatives in their lives, a group of individuals wanting a job, but more abstractly, solutions to their personal problems. Murkoff's prose style is gorgeous in its precise, metaphor-rich shimmer.

Scott, Walter.
Waverley. **1814.** Oxford. paper. 456pp. ISBN 0-19-283601-3.

Considered to be the first historical novel, *Waverley* was originally published anonymously. It is set in England and Scotland in the critical year 1745, in which the Stuart pretender to the British throne was finally dismissed by events on a bloody battlefield. The specific focus is on a young soldier in the English forces, sent north to suppress the Stuart uprising, who becomes involved in the cause himself. Politics and culture are depicted in great detail.

The Corridors of Power

These novels offer glimpses into the seats of power, where decisions affecting the entire citizenry, good or bad, are made.

Enquist, Per Olov.
The Royal Physician's Visit. **2001.** Overlook. 314pp. ISBN 1-58567-196-7; Washington Square. paper. 320pp. ISBN 0-7434-5803-6.

Offering a compelling view into a time and place rarely, if ever, visited in fiction available to American readers, this novel by a distinguished Swedish writer explores the cold, calculating, eighteenth-century court of Denmark's deranged king, Christian VII, where a German doctor holds sway over monarch and country, introducing many needed reforms but also setting into motion his own demise.

Falconer, Colin.
When We Were Gods: A Novel of Cleopatra. **2000.** Three Rivers. paper. 503pp. ISBN 0-609-80889-3.

Falconer captures the famous Egyptian queen as we know her: beautiful, politically wise, and making her own way through history. She was assailed from all sides—from within and outside the country—all during her reign, and for the good of Egypt and herself as its ruler, she enlisted, by means of passion and sexuality, the men who most mattered at the time in her part of the world: the Romans Julius Caesar and Mark Antony. Diplomacy and intrigue and the gilded trappings of Hellenic Egypt occupy center stage in this long but fast-paced novel about a fascinating time and place.

McCullough, Colleen.
Caesar's Women. **1994.** Avon. paper. 943pp. ISBN 0-380-71084-6.

A companion to the author's *Caesar*, another volume in her <u>Masters of Rome</u> series, this novel rivets our attention on the women who influenced the great Roman leader's life and who, in turn, saw their own lives forever marked by his presence, personality, and power. What Caesar said, went, and how such a one-person show was constituted and accomplished is revealed here.

Plaidy, Jean.
The Captive of Kensington Palace. **1976.** Fawcett. paper. 288pp. ISBN 0-449-23413-4.
The Queen and Lord M. **1977.** Fawcett. paper. 268pp. ISBN 0-449-23605-6.
The Queen's Husband. **1978.** Fawcett. paper. 382pp. ISBN 0-449-23896-2.

Plaidy is one of the most prolific historical novelists, and her brand of historical fiction leans toward the romantic. Her series about Queen Victoria is distinctive because, despite a great deal of nonfiction having been written about this great monarch, very little historical fiction has taken her up as a subject. These three volumes follow Victoria from her childhood and young womanhood under the strict control of her mother, the duchess of Kent, through her early years as queen, influenced by her prime minister, Lord Melbourne, to her marriage to the man who consumed her, Prince Albert. A constitutional monarch in the making; a constitutional monarchy profiled.

Richaud, Frederic.
Gardener to the King. **2001.** Arcade. 117pp. ISBN 1-55970-583-3.

As Louis XIV's efforts to secure France's supremacy rage across Europe, upsetting and unsettling every other country and ruler and the balance of power, the Sun King's gardener at the Palace of Versailles quietly rules his own domain. An unusual perspective on the pomp and ceremony of the lavish French court at the apogee of the ancien regime is here delivered in succinct and beautiful prose. Despite the ostensible narrowness of the novel's focus, a whole universe—Louis's world and dynamic character—emerges as resonantly as if the novel were 500 pages long.

Tremain, Rose.
Restoration. **1990.** Penguin. paper. 371pp. ISBN 0-14-012893-X.

With the restoration of the British monarchy in 1660 after more than a decade of Puritan severity, Charles II and the country itself faced life with new exuberance. By way of Tremain's invention of the delightful Robert Merivel, veterinarian to the king and then husband-of-convenience to the royal mistress, the tones and hues of this especially colorful time are spellbindingly evoked: from lavish court life to the dreadful plague decimating the population.

Vidal, Gore.
Hollywood. **1990.** Vintage. paper. 484pp. ISBN 0-375-70875-8.

From the White House, where President Woodrow Wilson must respond to the great conflagration consuming Europe, to the offices of the newspaper magnate William Randolph Hearst, to the early movie studios of Hollywood (from where the social impact of that exciting new medium continued to grow in depth and pervasiveness), esteemed writer Vidal engages in his trademark detailed but elegant prose as he continues, in this entry in his American Chronicle series, to chart the growth of the major bases of power and influence in American culture.

A Long, Long Time Ago

Creative novelists have no problem imagining life before recorded history.

Auel, Jean M.
The Clan of the Cave Bear. **1980.** Bantam. paper. 495pp. ISBN 0-553-25042-6.

With this novel, the author not only inaugurated her extremely popular Earth's Children series, but also almost single-handedly invented the subgenre of prehistorical fiction. In the time of the Ice Age, when the human species was in its infancy, love and protectiveness and compassion transcended clashes between radically different tribes. It is Auel's talent to conjure the terrain and environment as perceived by the eye and brain so long ago, not how we would see things today.

Auel, Jean M.
The Shelters of Stone. **2002.** Bantam. paper. 895pp. ISBN 0-553-28942-X.

This is the fifth and latest of the author's Earth's Children novels set in prehistoric times (see *The Clan of the Cave Bear,* above). Auel's copious research and fertile imagination build a world so replete with, so populated by, characters with both authentic period mindset and contemporary interest, that this novel and the others in the series educate as well as entertain.

Gear, Kathleen O'Neal, and Michael Gear.
People of the Moon. **2005.** Forge. 528pp. ISBN 0-765-30856-8.

The thirteenth installment in the Gears' First North Americans series of prehistorical novels, begun with *People of the Wolf* (see below), is one of the most effective in terms of both the Gears' understanding of early Native American life and the sheer excitement and rapid pace of the narrative. In an area of North America that is now northern New Mexico and southern Colorado, the Chaco Anasazi have controlled the region and its various peoples for 200 years. But a warrior, Ripple, begins an insurrection against the oppressive practices of the hated conquering tribe. Reading about the violence of battle and especially the torture practiced at that time is almost impossible to bear, but it is all part of the authors' insistence on realism.

Gear, Kathleen O'Neal, and Michael Gear.
People of the Owl. **2003.** Forge. paper. 640pp. ISBN 0-8125-8983-1.

With the authors' marked ability to marshal considerable detail and render it into a dynamic narrative, this installment in the Gears's popular First North Americans series reconstructs domestic life and "foreign affairs" of the aboriginal people of what is now northeastern Louisiana. The intensely instructive nature of this visit to past cultures—an out-and-out education, but an easily palatable one—is the calling card of this novel and, for that matter, the entire series.

Gear, Kathleen O'Neal, and Michael Gear.
People of the Wolf. **1990.** Tor. paper. 464pp. ISBN 0-7653-5030-0.

The authors mine the same vein as the staggeringly popular Jean Auel, writing extremely detailed but most definitely edifying and compelling dramas set in prehistoric times. In this inaugural volume in the Gears's First North Americans series, a band of resilient people migrate across the frozen bridge between the old world and a vast, new, unspoiled world. An extremely atmospheric depiction; readers feel the cold and experience the wonderment of discovering a new place.

Golding, William.
The Inheritors. **1955.** Harvest. paper. 233pp. ISBN 0-15-644379-1.

An enticing, highly creative novel about Neanderthals—not rude, crude men who are slovenly and disrespectful toward women (as in modern usage) but the prehistoric forerunners to *Homo sapiens*. This British Nobel laureate, best known for his seminal novel *Lord of the Flies*, astonishes readers with his perception of how primitive humans would think as he works out his theme of humankind's inherent evil by pitting the innocent Neanderthals against the corrupt, more intelligent human species that ultimately succeeded them.

Jennings, Gary.
Aztec. **1980.** Tor. paper. 1,056pp. ISBN 0-8125-2146-3.
Aztec Autumn. **1997.** Tor. paper. 480pp. ISBN 0-8125-9096-1.
Aztec Blood. **2001.** Tor. paper. 750pp. ISBN 0-8125-9098-8.

In each novel, Jennings focuses on a main character who, although fictional, serves to exemplify, reflect, and illustrate the harsh, even cruel tenor of life in Aztec culture, from the height of the empire's power, to its decline at the hands of the Spanish conquistadors, to the installment of tight, even brutal, control by the imperial overlord from Europe, to its guise as a province called New Spain. Extensively researched, these novels present history accurately and with a professional sense of how to compose a compelling narrative.

Exotic Locales

Just as travel literature can, historical novels can sweep readers off to exciting places where they have never been before, without leaving their armchairs, but all is not always well upon arrival at their destinations.

Clarke, Austin.
The Polished Hoe. **2003.** HarperCollins. 480pp. ISBN 0-06-055565-3; Amistad. paper. 480pp. ISBN 0-06-055762-1.

Setting his novel in the West Indies in the 1930s and 1940s, Canadian (Barbados-born) Clarke lets May-Matilda, an old woman living on a sugar plantation, tell her own story as she confesses to committing a major crime but also, as she gives in to reminiscence, chart the history and recall the tenor of plantation life as she knew it in colonial days. While palm trees swayed, May-Matilda was the long-term victim of racism, servitude, and sexual exploitation.

Clavell, James.
Tai-Pan. **1966.** Dell. paper. 736pp. ISBN 0-440-18462-2.

In this novel the author, whose name is synonymous with sagas that are long but nevertheless exciting, crowded with characters and detail but compelling just the same, takes his readers to the port of Hong Kong in the 1840s. Naturally, since that British colony's raison d'être has always been trade, trade is the theme of this luxuriously detailed exploration of the conflicts between those who trade in tea and those who trade in opium.

Han Bangqing.
The Sing-Song Girls of Shanghai. **1894.** Columbia University. 556pp. ISBN 0-231-12268-3.

With so many characters to keep straight and a choppy, highly episodic narrative, this is a novel only the dedicated and careful literary fiction reader will enjoy. That said, the many characters populate a world the reader will be amazed to visit. The novel was published in the author's native China, where he was a highly regarded literary figure; it has now (in 2005) been translated into English. Shanghai bears an exotic reputation, and the author locates his heavily populated and deeply textured novel in the so-called pleasure quarters of that atmospheric city in the late nineteenth century. They weren't haphazard little dens of iniquity, but rather recognized institutions catering to responsible, established men. As well as the author shows understanding of the many characters, it is his comprehension of this particular milieu that makes this novel stand out.

Nguyen, Kien.
Le Colonial. **2004.** Little, Brown. 320pp. ISBN 0-316-28501-3.

This Vietnamese writer takes readers back to the late eighteenth century, when his country was called Annam. Through the three French missionaries' efforts to convert the local people, he paints a lush picture of that country—elegant temples, verdant forests, beautiful mountains in the distance one would want to capture in watercolor—at the beginning of a terrible civil war. The horror of widespread violence is ironically borne on poetic prose.

Phillips, Caryl.
Cambridge. **1992.** Random. paper. 192pp. ISBN 0-679-73689-1.

By a distinguished English writer, this is a riveting, richly dimensional picture of black slavery, achieved by juxtaposing narratives told by two very dissimilar individuals whose lives nevertheless intersect: a young Englishman in the nineteenth century, sent to the West Indies to look over his father's sugar plantation and there faced with heat and racial tension; and a black slave named Cambridge who works on the plantation. The clash of the grim realities of human life set amid lush surroundings is intentionally disturbing.

Rhys, Jean.
The Wide Sargasso Sea. **1966**. Penguin. paper. 192pp. ISBN 0-14-018983-1.

Rhys was born and raised on the West Indian island of Dominica, but most of her novels are set in Europe, to which she emigrated as a teenager, contemporaneous to the time in which they were written (the 1930s). However, this one, generally considered her masterpiece, takes place in her native Caribbean region, and it is a poetic, concise, deeply sensual, rigorously psychological, vastly creative, and completely engrossing imagining of the early life of a young Creole woman who eventually becomes a famous fictional character we never actually meet, the mad first Mrs. Rochester in Charlotte Brontë's classic novel *Jane Eyre*. The provenance of her mental distress is seen in large part in her inability to secure a footing in either the black or white communities on the island. Beneath the swaying of the palms, above the rhythmic pounding of the surf, lies racial violence. The lasting resonance of this novel is its sobering picture of an earthly paradise.

Rice, Anne.
The Feast of All Saints. **1979**. Ballantine. paper. 640pp. ISBN 0-375-33453-1.

With her typical eye for generous and telling detail, Rice explores a fascinating city—New Orleans—and a particularly fascinating aspect of New Orleans history, the *gens de couleur libres*, the free people of color, springing from both black and white worlds and tenuously suspended between the two. This population was unique in the South before the Civil War, where usually anyone of black African heritage was in bondage. "Of course the gens de couleur posed a special problem and always had. Well bred and educated. . . . But how could one account for their living here generation after generation in a country and a region that did not want them, that would never permit them equality, and sought ultimately to crush their heads?" Riveting in its narrative drive and unforgettable for what the reader learns about this milieu.

Smiley, Jane.
The Greenlanders. **1989**. Anchor. paper. 608pp. ISBN 1-4000-9546-8.

The Iowa of Smiley's 1991 career-cresting novel *A Thousand Acres*, for which she won the Pulitzer Prize, is far removed from the time and place this novel securely assumes as its setting: fourteenth-century Greenland. Smiley is obviously at home here and makes the reader equally so. She adheres to the traditional epic form in which Old Norse sagas were composed: multigenerational in scope and heroic in tone. Her characters—the family of farmer Gunnar Asgeirsson—breathe as real-life people and suffer harsh conditions (illness and hearts hardened by unhappiness) like we do, but the most resonant quality of this vastly absorbing novel is the setting: the "hunger and storms and freezing" are bleak, to be sure.

Vargas Llosa, Mario.
The Way to Paradise. **2003.** Picador. paper. 400pp. ISBN 0-312-42403-5.

The great Peruvian master of fiction once again demonstrates why historical fiction is so highly regarded in Latin America—from the genre's popularity with the general reading public to the serious attention given it by critics to the active and enthusiastic participation in the writing of historical novels by intensely literary figures such as Vargas Llosa. This is a dual biography of Paul Gauguin, able to completely express his artistic sensibilities in the open, gorgeous South Pacific (lush Tahiti), and his grandmother, a formidable women's—and workers'—rights activist. Ocean breezes versus dark factories—which would you prefer?

White, Jenny.
The Sultan's Seal. **2005.** Norton. 384pp. ISBN 0-393-06099-3.

This very accomplished first novel is obviously derived from and rests securely on the author's background as a professor of anthropology and author of several nonfiction books on Turkish social and political life, which is not to say that her fictional foray into Turkey's past—the declining days of the Ottoman Empire in the late nineteenth century—is dryly academic; far from it. This is a richly detailed but at the same time fluidly unfolded story about the death of a young Englishwoman, the governess to the former sultan's granddaughter, whose body is found naked with the sultan's seal on a chain around her neck. Evenly and compelling plotted, and with carefully drawn characters, it is nevertheless the setting of old Istanbul that remains in the mind: center of a polyglot empire, seething with intrigue as the paranoid sultan spies on everyone.

The World's Great Cities

Often the city in which a historical novel takes place, because of the dexterous, atmospheric, and even exciting way the author paints it, becomes the novel's predominant feature.

Ackroyd, Peter.
The Clerkenwell Tales. **2004.** Doubleday/Nan A. Talese. 244pp. ISBN 0-385-51121-3; Avon. paper. 224pp. ISBN 1-4000-7595-5.

Late medieval London—dirty, smelly, disease-ridden—is cast here as more than just a vivid backdrop for a rollicking novel that follows the characters who made appearances in *The Canterbury Tales*. Writing with the pace and tone of a thriller, Ackroyd has great fun testing the religious and political natures of the English capital, seething with plots and intrigue, including the probable deposition of the king, Richard II, by the usurping Duke of Lancaster (who will succeed in his endeavor and become King Henry IV); a prioress with a problem nun on her hands; and a band of violent heretics.

Makiya, Kanan.
The Rock: A Tale of Seventeenth-Century Jerusalem. **2001.** Pantheon. 368pp. ISBN 0-375-40087-7; Vintage. paper. 368pp. ISBN 0-375-70078-1.

> The Rock of Jerusalem is an essential symbol for three religions: Judaism, Christianity, and Islam. It is where Abraham attempted to sacrifice his son, Isaac; where the temple of Solomon stood; where Jesus preached; and where Muhammad ascended to heaven. This fascinating and even educational novel investigates the Rock's importance to these faiths, and how the three religions used to get along in former days, through the story of the son of an advisor to the caliph and a Jewish convert to Islam, who designed the mosque called the Dome of the Rock.

Riviere, William.
By the Grand Canal. **2005.** Grove. 272pp. ISBN 0-8021-1793-7.

> From the author of *Kate Caterina* comes another historical novel set in Italy. Events in the previous novel took place just before and during World War II; this novel locates its action in Venice immediately after World War I. The focus is a British diplomat involved in the peace conference in Paris, who neglects his family back in England, but the Venice itself takes the driver's seat in this novel, in all its exceptional, chimerical beauty and its ability, because of its loveliness and timeliness, to elevate one's outlook on life.

Rutherfurd, Edward.
London. **1997.** Ballantine. paper. 1,152pp. ISBN 0-345-45568-1.

> Rutherfurd is known for effectively condensing thousands of years of history into a thousand-page novel, and this one shows him at work—but, so it seems, not *hard* at work, for such a task appears easy in his dexterous hands, if readability is the measure by which this author's sweat is judged. As is his usual method of operation, in this novel Rutherford follows the fortunes of a handful of families—in this case, residents in the British capital—whose generations embody the rise and fall of social, political, and economic trends and eras, with the great city looming overhead. If cities can dominate life and predominate as a feature in a novel, then London is the Green Giant, triumphing over all other cities, with the possible exception of New York City.

Stockley, Phillippa.
A Factory of Cunning. **2005.** Harcourt. 384pp. ISBN 0-15-101172-9.

> Through a series of letters, the physical roughness and deceit, passion, and ruthlessness of life in eighteenth-century London are explored as the author maneuvers a self-exiled French noblewoman and her maid through high society, trying to secure a place there. Calling themselves Mrs. Fox and Victoria, their adventures—and deception—lead from mansion to country house, and lead readers on a delightful romp through sexual dalliances and social machinations.

Place as the Main Character

Some historical novelists are so good at establishing place in the reader's mind that it becomes the chief character in the book.

Blain, Michael.
The Midnight Band of Mercy. **2004.** Soho. 384pp. ISBN 1-56947-371-4.
New York City in the 1890s, from what people wore to how they spoke, and specifically the tenor of a big-city newsroom in that era, springs vividly to life in this murky, mysterious, compelling novel about a freelance reporter hot on the trail of juicy material about scandals in the Catholic Church. Everywhere the reader turns in this book, there is New York, looming big and bustling over the narrative.

Chwin, Stefan.
Death in Danzig. **2004.** Harcourt. 256pp. ISBN 0-15-100805-1.
After World War II, the German city of Danzig became the Polish city of Gdansk. During the last year of the war (1945), the German residents fled as the Russian army gained control of the city and Poles were seeking refuge there. This city—a truly cosmopolitan place, a crossroad of cultures and armies that have marked the history of central Europe—is defined in its new identity by the blood of its old and new inhabitants; despite the specific and compelling stories the author tells about individuals, it is the city itself that occupies center stage.

Kelly, Thomas.
Empire Rising. **2005.** Farrar. 400pp. ISBN 0-374-14781-5.
The construction of the Empire State Building in New York City is the historical occasion upon which the author builds this robust novel. Despite the thriller-like plot line, sturdily built characters, and a vivid capturing of the immigrant and political life that dominated the city's climate at that time, it is nevertheless the Big Apple itself—as it was the "context" for the erection of this magnificent structure—that remains with the reader, standing as the capital of the world that it was and remains.

Michener, James A.
Hawaii. **1959.** Ballantine. paper. 1,036pp. ISBN 0-449-21335-8.
Michener is the über-historical novelist when it comes to spinning long, completely enveloping storylines focused on a particular geographical location. The prefatory note in this, one of his most popular works, says, "This is a novel." Yes, indeed, but it is so much more than that; it is an education (as are all of his novels) in the geographical, historical, and cultural evolution and development of—in this case—the Hawaiian Islands. One learns a lot from

Michener, but the easy, even pace guarantees that the reader does not experience a sensation of being lectured to. Others of his oeuvre to enjoy include *The Source*, *The Covenant*, and *Centennial*.

Pamuk, Orhan.
My Name Is Red. **2001.** Knopf. 448pp. ISBN 0-375-40695-6; Vintage. paper. 432pp. ISBN 0-375-70685-2.

This Turkish novelist enjoys a broadening international reputation, and this magnificently absorbing novel testifies to his prodigious talent. In the sixteenth-century Ottoman Empire, the Sultan commissions a book of self-celebration, and a group of artists is assembled to illustrate it. From alternating points of view, the author takes the reader to an intellectual murder mystery (with riveting discussion of the nature of art), but ultimately the novel is a delicious portrait of the palaces and byways and deadly intrigue rampant in the great Ottoman capital, Istanbul.

Saramago, José.
Baltasar and Blimunda. **1982.** Harvest. paper. 360pp. ISBN 0-15-600520-4.

The 1998 winner of the Nobel Prize in Literature typically writes discursive, ruminative novels that display the author's extensive knowledge of history, culture, and human behavior, but at the same time his novels are highly compelling for their colorful characters and wonderful storylines, and this novel is no exception. It is set in eighteenth-century Portugal, at the height of the Inquisition, and it is an enchantingly conceived epic about royal power, religion, and love, all rendered in an entertaining blend of realism and mysticism. Ultimately, though, it is dark and devout Portugal itself that emerges as the central character.

Chapter 2

Character

"I just finished a novel based on the life of King Henry VIII of England, and now I want to read another one about some other colorful, strong ruler." This is certainly not an out-of-line request made to a readers' advisory librarian. After setting and story, character is a readily apparent and easily identifiable factor of how historical fiction is both defined and enjoyed by the reader and explained by the reader to a librarian. Character is undoubtedly one of the primary motivations compelling a writer to venture into writing historical fiction in the first place: the intriguing idea of pumping new life into a historical figure or creating one that is entirely fictitious but nevertheless true to his or her setting.

But again, as in the chapter on setting, a listing of novels all about Henry VIII, or American first ladies, is helpful but certainly not unique or hard to find. Why not link historical novels that emphasize character over setting or story in new, beguiling ways, guiding readers from a certain "type" of character to others of that type but with the circumstances surrounding the characters different—in other words, taking readers on a visit with similar types of characters in entirely, often vastly, different settings?

Royalty Rules

Come, walk with kings. . . . Approaching and appreciating the colorful lives of crowned heads is entirely permissible and completely encouraged here.

Davis, Kathryn.
Versailles. **2002.** Back Bay. paper. 206pp. ISBN 0-316-73761-5.

The soul of the unfortunate Queen Marie Antoinette of France shares intimate remembrances and vivid impressions of the history of her marriage to Louis XVI, and, more resonantly, she remembers all the sounds, smells, and textures of the immense palace she adored and called home. In this graceful novel, the queen with such a bad reputation is given substance beyond her simple desire to have fun.

Harrison, Kathryn.
Poison. **1996.** Avon. paper. 317pp. ISBN 0-380-72741-2.

A beautifully detailed, sensuous, intelligent but appropriately psychologically dark return to seventeenth-century Spain, where lines of comparison are provocatively drawn between the lives of two young, beleaguered women from different walks of life: the daughter of a failed silkworm grower, who is accused of witchcraft; and Queen Maria Luisa, who cannot fulfill her duty as the king's consort: to conceive a needed heir to the throne.

Mann, Heinrich.
Young Henry of Navarre. **1935.** Overlook. paper. 585pp. ISBN 1-58567-487-7.
Henry, King of France. **1936.** Overlook. paper. 786pp. ISBN 1-58567-488-5.

The brother of the more famous (and Nobel Prize–winning) German writer Thomas Mann tills an extremely rich historical field in this two-part epic, a seriously researched and vibrantly and dramatically written depiction, which, in the first volume, traces the early life and path to the throne of one of France's best and best-loved monarchs, Henry IV, founder of the Bourbon dynasty. The second volume shows him as king, facing consequential religious issues but interrupted in his efforts by assassination.

Min, Anchee.
Empress Orchid. **2004.** Houghton. 352pp. ISBN 0-618-06887-2.

According to accepted wisdom, the collapse of the Chinese imperial monarchy in 1912 was due in no small part to the selfishness and tyranny of the infamous dowager empress, Tzu Hsi, or Orchid. But this lavish novel paints a more rounded, or at least less sharp-edged, portrait as Min explores the dowager empress's early life in the elaborately ritualized and demeaning system of concubinage behind the secretive walls of Peking's Forbidden City.

Plaidy, Jean.
Mary, Queen of France. **1964.** Random/Three Rivers. paper. 295pp. ISBN 0-609-81021-9.
The Thistle and the Rose. **1973.** Random/Three Rivers. paper. 316pp. ISBN 0-609-81022-7.

Plaidy, one of the most prolific historical fiction novelists of all time, was the pen name of Eleanor Hibbert. These two titles are part of her Tudor

<u>Princesses</u> series, which picture the lives, in a definitely romantic light but with careful historical accuracy, of Henry VIII's two strong sisters. One,the queen consort of Louis XII of France, turns from political pawn into political player, and the other, queen consort of James IV of Scotland, also stakes out a power base.

Tarr, Judith.
Queen of Swords. **1997.** Tor. paper. 464pp. ISBN 0-312-86805-7.

A prolific historical novelist, Tarr here takes readers to an uncommon setting: the twelfth-century Holy Land, and the intrigue-soaked court of Melisande, queen of Jerusalem, strong-willed ruler of one of the Crusader kingdoms. This vibrant tale is told through the eyes of a fictional French-woman, Lady Richildis, who ventures east on a pilgrimage and becomes an attendant to the queen. This is a story of royalty always on the defensive, never allowed to develop permanent roots.

A Large but Well-Drawn Cast

These novels are populated by many characters, all of whom emerge as more than just two-dimensional stick figures.

Day, Cathy.
The Circus in Winter. **2004.** Harcourt. 288pp. ISBN 0-15-101048-X.

These eleven linked short stories amount to a multifaceted novel as the author limns the lives of circus people and their offspring, from the 1880s to the late 1930s. A small Indiana town extends itself as the winter home of the Great Porter Circus, and in turn the circus extends itself as the home of a pas-sel of extremely colorful characters, including Jennie, who does a "Spin of Death" act; Ollie, a retired clown; and Bascomb and Pearly, hus-band-and-wife "pinheads."

Diamant, Anita.
The Last Days of Dogtown. **2005.** Scribner. 288pp. ISBN 0-7432-2573-2.

The author set her best-selling novel *The Red Tent* (1997) in biblical times; in her third novel, she brings her story forward considerably. Still, even though it is set as "recently" as the early years of the nineteenth century, this novel clearly is another of her immaculate reconstructions of the social mores at play in a certain place and time in the past. The reader has been de-posited in the Massachusetts town of Cape Ann in the early 1800s. The com-munity (nicknamed "Dogtown") is expiring, and its death throes are documented by the last remaining residents, who are too reluctant or unable to relocate and who dominate the narrative here, each weaving his or her voice into the tapestry. Among them are Black Ruth, the female stonemason who meets the world in male attire; and Judy Rivers, who is white and is having an affair with a free slave, which would scandalize the town if it became known. A realistic and ultimately sad tale.

Doctorow, E. L.
The March. **2005.** Random. 372pp. ISBN 0-375-50671-3.

This highly esteemed American fiction writer, a perennial examiner of the culture of his country, turns to history to lay open the roots of the state of our contemporary society (which he did most famously in *Ragtime*). The march referred to in the title is a notorious one: General William T. Sherman's march through Georgia and the Carolinas in the declining years of the Civil War. Doctorow, following the usual formula of historical novels about wars and battles, uses historical figures supported by inventions of his own, and the amalgam is particularly smooth. These wrought-in-depth "made-up" characters include the brave daughters of a slave and slave owner, the equally strong daughter of a Southern judge, and a freed slave destined to be a war photographer.

Durham, David Anthony.
Pride of Carthage. **2005.** Doubleday. 656pp. ISBN 0-385-50603-1.

An accomplished, even exciting, retelling of the second Punic War. Hannibal Barca, the great Carthaginian general, is determined to thwart the growing Roman Empire and to sack the great city itself. He is the focus of this detailed and dynamic narrative, and Durham gives him admirable roundness. But the author also develops a strong supporting cast, which includes Hannibal's brothers as well as less prominent figures making up Carthage's grand movement against its archenemy.

McMurtry, Larry.
Lonesome Dove. **1985.** Pocket. paper. 945pp. ISBN 0-671-68390-X.

McMurtry's ever-popular novel set a high-water mark not only in his career but also for novels attempting realistic and even captivating re-creation of the Old West. This vast, rich panorama is exemplary in accuracy and energy and won the Pulitzer Prize. The framework upon which McMurtry weaves his tale is a cattle drive from Texas to Montana in 1876. His talent is most obvious in his ability to breathe new life into stock Western characters, from Indians to the infamous lady with a heart of gold, breaking through the romantic myth of the Old West to depict fully dimensional, *real* people.

Merezhkovskii, Dmitri.
The Death of the Gods. **1896.** Kessinger. paper. 464pp. ISBN 0-7661-0114-2.

This classic novel by a Russian writer shared its setting with Gore Vidal's later *Julian*: that is, the fourth-century reign of the Roman emperor Julian. It has been credited for its remarkable ability to infuse great viability—and distinctive, individual traits—into numerous characters, from soldiers in the Roman legion to little children running wild in the streets of Constantinople to fawning court members surrounding the great Caesar himself. These characters effectively dramatize *the* great drama of the time: the clash between paganism and Christianity. Julian is an intelligent man, at home in the conflicting philosophies of the day, but he prefers the pagan gods to the Christian one whose worship his grandfather, Emperor Constantine, had declared the official religion of the empire. Emphasized here is the military campaign that Julian waged against the Persians to show the citizens of the Eastern Roman Empire that he and his beliefs were to be respected—with personally fatal results.

Rutherfurd, Edward.
The Princes of Ireland: The Dublin Saga: Book One. **2004.** Ballantine. paper. 816pp. ISBN 0-345-47235-7.

Like James Michener, an American a generation older than he, this British writer specializes in highly detailed narratives that, with the personalizing effect of a large assortment of viably "human" characters, reconstruct the entire history of a place. In this case, that place is Ireland, the book's focal point being the Irish capital, Dublin. This title is the first volume in a proposed two-volume set that will recall and relive seventeen centuries of Irish history. Color, sweep, and drama are all manifested through the lives of many vibrant characters, including chieftains, Druids, Vikings, noblemen, and monks.

Scott, Sir Walter.
Kenilworth. **1821.** Penguin. paper. 528pp. ISBN 0-14-043654-5.

Ever-popular Scott, credited with being the originator of the historical novel, set this one not in his native Scotland but in England, in the year 1575. It centers on an actual set of circumstances: the marriage of Queen Elizabeth I's favorite, Lord Dudley, to Amy Robsart, and her subsequent death under mysterious circumstances. As always with Scott, the novel boasts richly drawn, deeply etched characters—including, in addition to the electric personality of the queen herself and the handsome, charming Lord Dudley, Richard Varney, who is Leicester's master of horse, and Edmund Teressilian, a friend of Amy Robsart.

Swerling, Beverly.
Shadowbrook: A Novel of Love, War, and the Birth of America. **2004.** Simon & Schuster. 592pp. ISBN 0-7432-2812-X; Simon & Schuster. paper. 512pp. ISBN 0-7432-2813-8.

Colonial America at the time of the French and Indian War provides a dramatic backdrop for this author's large cast of characters. The setting is the Ohio Country, hotbed of conflicting English and French claims to the western dominion beyond the colonies. This is a character-rich and -driven novel, each character individually and forcefully drawn. The primary characters in the stable of brightly painted individuals are Quentin Hale, who owns a sprawling estate in upstate New York and is a guide to Virginia surveyor and colonel George Washington; Cormac Shea, Quentin's friend, half Indian and half Irish; and Nicole Crane, a young Frenchwoman and Quentin's love interest.

Vidal, Gore.
The Golden Age. **2000.** Vintage. paper. 480pp. ISBN 0-375-72481-8.

From World War II to the cold war, brilliant historical novelist Vidal brings his <u>American Chronicle</u> series one step closer to contemporary times. Politics predominates in this novel: the processes and individuals peculiar to the American way of government during this time. But, as always, the influence that journalism wields in reflecting—even shaping—American life is also a major thread. Also as always in Vidal's novels, and even more so in this novel than in some other volumes in the series, he demonstrates his robust yet immaculate talent for mixing actual figures and fictional ones and making them all come alive, the former including FDR and media tycoon William Randolph Hearst, the latter newspaper publisher Caroline Sanford and journalist Peter Sanford.

Women with True Grit

These ladies plow through trouble and setbacks to get what they want and need.

Acevado, Chantel.
Love and Ghost Letters. **2005.** St. Martin's. 320pp. ISBN 0-312-34046-X.

Acevado's languid, sensual prose suits the atmosphere of the locale in which it is set—Cuba—that hung over the island in the presocialist days before the advent of Castro. Josefina, daughter of a wealthy man, has been raised with privilege, but poverty and loneliness are her lot after she runs off with a man not of her class. Her husband finds himself rarely at home because there Josefina is raising two children in a hardscrabble existence. Her story is poignantly rendered, never given to maudlin overtones. The author endows her attractive strength of character.

De Witt, Abigail.
Lili. **2000.** TriQuarterly. 304pp. ISBN 0-8101-5100-6; Norton. paper. 320pp. ISBN 0-393-32318-8.

In pre–World War I provincial France, young Lili grows up a spirited person, but when the war comes Lili must adapt to a more profane world than that she had known. Her soldier cousin is killed in the fighting and her soldier brother kills himself; she loses her faith. After the war, she experiences a difficult romance and marriage. The next world war strains her reserves and resources, but she emerges stronger and more self-identified.

Diamant, Anita.
> *The Red Tent.* **1997.** St. Martin's. 413pp. ISBN 0-312-18415-8; Picador. paper. 336pp. ISBN 0-312-19551-6.

> This immensely popular novel helped inaugurate a subgenre of fictional biographies of biblical women. This one is about Dinah, who is briefly referred to in the Book of Genesis as the daughter of Jacob. Diamant gives Dinah an authentic voice with which to tell her story. Through that story readers come to understand and appreciate women's roles and the community of women in the ancient Near East, especially the red tent, where they go once a month, give birth, and share tales and stories.

Diliberto, Gioia.
> *I Am Madame X.* **2003.** Scribner. 272pp. ISBN 0-7432-1155-3; Scribner. paper. 261pp. ISBN 0-7434-5680-7.

> Little is known about the woman—Virginie Gantreau—who posed for John Singer Sargent's beguiling and controversial painting *Portrait of Madame X.* So biographer Diliberto turns to fiction to flesh out a compelling portrait. Virginie's beauty was her calling card as she made her way from man to man, from her native Louisiana (she was of Creole stock) to the France of the Second Empire and the Belle Époque, from child to capricious, vain, but complex woman of extraordinary beauty.

Jong, Erica.
> *Sappho's Leap.* **2003.** Norton. 320pp. ISBN 0-393-05761-5; Norton. paper. 316pp. ISBN 0-393-32561-X.

> The "poetess" (to use an outdated, not politically correct term) of ancient Greece is brought to mesmerizing life by the author of the famous novel *Fear of Flying* (1973), herself also a poet. Apparently few facts are known about Sappho, but that limitation does not stop Jong, who creatively takes what is available and spins a provocatively conceived, intelligent, and gorgeously written fictional portrait of this adventurous, sensual, and confident woman.

Learner, Tobsha.
> *The Witch of Cologne.* **2005.** Tor/Forge. paper. ISBN 0-765-31430-4.

> The popularity of *The Red Tent,* by Anita Diamant, and *Sarah,* by Marek Halter, is a good indication that a sizable readership exists for novels about strong Jewish women from the past. In that same vein is this fictional account of a seventeenth-century woman named Ruth, a midwife well versed in her trade (as well as Kabbalah) yet subject to and refusing to be a victim of religious and gender prejudice. Ruth is the 20-something daughter of a rabbi in Cologne, Germany, and the novel's title more than suggests what the local Catholic inquisitor accuses the intelligent Ruth of being; however, she is not about to buckle under these accusations. These were intellectually curious

and questioning times, but at the same time narrowmindedness was not absent. Ruth, upright and brave, is caught in the middle.

Morgan, Jude.
Passion: A Novel of the Romantic Poets. **2005.** St. Martin's. 544pp. ISBN 0-312-34368-X.

Byron, Shelley, and Keats—the great triumvirate of English Romantic poets. Their interesting lives and revolutionary work, by definition, provide excellent fodder for not only the art of biography but also the historical novel, and Morgan takes up the "assignment" well. The women in these men's lives—Lady Caroline Lamb, Lord Byron's obsessive lover; Mary Shelley, the intellectual and author of the classic novel *Frankenstein*; Fanny Brawne, a name not widely recognized these days but the inspiration behind many of Keats's poems; and last but not least, Augusta Leigh, Byron's half-sister and inappropriate love-object—are brought strongly into the picture as well. In fact, it is through their eyes and consciousness that the lives of the three poets are recalled. These are convention-defying women, and Morgan portrays them with sparkling individuality but also within the context of the circumscribed conditions in which women lived in the nineteenth century.

Piercy, Marge.
City of Darkness, City of Light. **1996.** Fawcett. Paper. 496pp. ISBN 0-449-91275-2.

Piercy's sensitivity to women's sensibilities comes to fruition in the historical fiction arena in this novel about three women significantly involved in the great tumult known as the French Revolution. Historically speaking, Claire Lacombe, Manon Philipan, and Pauline Leon may stand in the shadows cast by their prominent male colleagues—Maximilian Robespierre, Georges Danton, and Nicholas Condorcet—but Piercy endows them with their own courage and importance and tells an authentic but also entertaining and bold tale that establishes the vital part women played in this world-altering event.

Poniatowska, Elena.
Here's to You, Jesusa! **1969.** Penguin, 2001. paper. 336pp. ISBN 0-14-200122-8.

Based on a historical figure from the pages of early twentieth-century Mexican history, of whom virtually no American readers will have heard, this novel (originally published in the author's native Mexico in 1969 and only recently translated into English) is a riveting depiction of women's place in society and politics in that setting. Jesusa, from the provinces, joins a cavalry unit during the Mexican Revolution; afterward, times *really* get tough! The husband she married (*not* by choice) is physically abusive, but his death—when she is only 18—is a release only in an immediate way, for now she is alone and adrift in the huge and unforgiving capital, Mexico City. But she's resilient, and she refuses to lie down and be trampled by poverty and the police. Jesusa works in various jobs, and each guise she assumes increases her independent spirit; she remains untrammeled.

Shu-Ching, Shih.

City of the Queen. **2005.** Columbia University. 288pp. ISBN 0-231-13456-8.

Now translated into English from the Chinese as well as condensed into a single volume, this three-novel cycle, known collectively as the Hong Kong trilogy, first appeared in the 1990s under three separate covers. It is a multigenerational saga, set in Hong Kong. The narrative begins in the 1880s, and the story continues over four generations of the same family up to when Britain handed over Hong Kong to the Chinese in the late 1990s. As the tale opens, 13-year-old Huang Deyun is kidnapped from the mainland and sold into slavery in colonial Hong Kong. In the course of a long and astonishingly successful life, she becomes a powerful businesswoman and matriarch of a clan that not only witnesses but reflects the transition of Hong Kong from an opium den, a backwater colony to an economic powerhouse brimming with glimmering high rises.

Undset, Sigrid.
Kristen Lavransdatter trilogy.

Kristen Lavransdatter, Vol. 1: The Bridal Wreath. **1920.** Penguin. paper. 336pp. ISBN 0-14-118041-2.

Kristen Lavransdatter, Vol. 2: The Mistress of Husaby. **1921.** Penguin. paper. 448pp. ISBN 0-14-118128-1.

Kristen Lavransdatter, Vol. 3: The Cross. **1922.** Penguin. paper. 464pp. ISBN 0-14-118235-0.

The three novels comprising this trilogy earned their Norwegian author the Nobel Prize for Literature in 1928. With these books Undset achieved international fame, and to this day the trilogy is fondly appreciated by historical fiction readers, who in these lush pages are taken to a time and place definitely not heavily mined in fiction: medieval Norway. The title character is an intrepid, willful, independent individual (with whom contemporary readers can readily identify) who, from childhood to mature womanhood, sets her own course in fifteenth-century Norway, pictured here in vividly created detail. She encounters many trials and tribulations during the progress of her difficult life; the reader is given is a marvelous mix of story, character, and setting.

The Writer's Plight

Sequestered in a cold-water garret somewhere, torturing body and soul in the search for fame and fortune—the romance of the writer's life holds special interest for many readers.

Cook, Bruce.
Young Will: The Confessions of William Shakespeare. **2004.** St. Martin's/Truman Talley. 416pp. ISBN 0-312-33573-3.

In his early fifties, the famous bard composes his memoirs, in which he seeks to assuage his guilt for his past sins. What emerges is a dark but delectable, fully human portrait of an individual who was by no means a saint. The life of a playwright in the soiled and grungy London of the sixteenth century is bracingly manifested.

Lodge, David.
Author, Author. **2004.** Viking. 390pp. ISBN 0-670-03349-9.

Irishman Tóibín's *The Master* (see below) imagines the life of the great American writer Henry James with great warmth and humanity. In this fictional version of that same life, English novelist and critic Lodge focuses his interest in James on the "Master's" unfortunate foray into playwriting. A genius, James is here endowed with endearing—to say nothing of enduring—flesh and blood.

Stead, C. K.
Mansfield. **2005.** Trafalgar Square. paper. 246pp. ISBN 0-099-46865-4.

This novel based on the life of the New Zealand master of the short story, Katherine Mansfield, a writer whose work continues to appear in every short story anthology, portrays what she was after in her fiction and in her personal relations, most notably with her husband, critic John Middleton Murray, and her friend and fellow writer, D. H. Lawrence. Mansfield died young, after years of suffering from tuberculosis, and what she went through to find relief from her symptoms while still managing to compose what has come to be regarded as classic literature is amazing.

Thornton, Lawrence.
Sailors on the Inward Sea. **2004.** Free Press. 288pp. ISBN 0-7432-6007-4.

This novel is presented in the form of a memoir written by a sailor and friend of Joseph Conrad, one of the giants of British literature. The memoir's author is called Jack Malone, and as Thornton has creatively imagined the situation, Malone served as the basis of Conrad's famous character Marlow. The novel includes great adventure as well as immaculate probing of the artistic mind: specifically, borrowing from real life material for fiction.

Tóibín, Colm.
The Master. **2004.** Scribner. 352pp. ISBN 0-7432-5040-2.

A distinguished Irish novelist injects the real-life character of great American literary icon Henry James, called by fellow writers the "Master," with considerable warmth and humanity. The specific era so eloquently explored here is James's later years, after his unwise venture into playwriting but before his great masterworks were published.

Life Stories in the Arts

Sensitive, creative individuals often lead lives different from those of other people—in many instances, more difficult lives because they suffer for their art. The story of their lives, their personal suffering and triumph, cannot fail to interest readers.

Basu, Kunal.
The Miniaturist. **2004.** Weidenfeld & Nicolson; dist. by Trafalgar Square. 247pp. ISBN 0-297-82926-2.

Sixteenth-century Hindustan under the Mughal Emperor Akbar, his imperial court swirling with violence and intrigue, is dazzlingly brought to light by way of the complicated and even tortured life of an artist who headed the court studio that produced the miniatures for which Mughal art is renowned. This artist's life-path is particularly intriguing for contemporary American readers, for whom it will be a brand-new journey.

Braver, Adam.
Divine Sarah. **2004.** Morrow. 224pp. ISBN 0-06-054407-4.

Braver artfully parallels the late careers of two quite different individuals whose lives intersected: the legendary actress Sarah Bernhardt, who paid a heavy price for her fame, relegated to lesser performance venues in her latest American tour and relying on opium for escape; and a tired newspaper reporter, unhappy that he has been assigned to cover her and about the course his career has taken. Two stories of personal frustration, rendered with careful nuance, absorbingly brought to light.

Chevalier, Tracy.
Girl with the Pearl Earring. **2000.** Plume. paper. 233pp. ISBN 0-452-28215-2.

The elegant simplicity of this novel's prose style evokes, first, life in seventeenth-century Delft, Holland, and second, the conditions in which Dutch master painter Johannes Vermeer created one of his incomparable masterpieces. The premise is that the activities in the Vermeer household are seen through the eyes of Griet, a maid. She begins helping her master mix his paints and ends up the model for his famous painting *Girl with the Pearl Earring*. Religious tensions (Griet is Protestant and the Vermeers Catholic) spark with sexual ones in this heartfelt story.

Doyle, Roddy.
Oh, Play That Thing. **2004.** Viking. 376pp. ISBN 0-670-03361-8.

Following his best-selling *A Star Called Henry*, Booker Prize–winning novelist and screenwriter Doyle submits a rigorously styled, passion-filled set of further adventures in the life of an Irish immigrant to 1920s New York and Chicago, who leaves behind—but can he?—his ex-IRA assassin past and eventually becomes trumpeter Louis Armstrong's right-hand man.

Rice, Anne.
Cry to Heaven. **1982.** Ballantine. paper. 566pp. ISBN 0-345-39693-6.

Life in the arts is more than hard work, it can involve downright mutilation, as witnessed by what these fellows went through. The deprived and at the same time gloriously indulgent lives of the eighteenth-century castrati, the altered male sopranos celebrated in the royal courts of Europe, are brilliantly resurrected here. One need not be an opera lover to fully enter this cruel but glorious world, unimaginable today, and to appreciate the peculiarity of the life stories of these men.

Steinke, Rene.
Holy Skirts. **2005.** Morrow. 368pp. ISBN 0-688-17694-1.

The author creates a fictionalized version of the life of a real-life poet and outrageous figure in Berlin and New York in the 1910s and 1920s, Baroness Elsa von Freytag-Loringhaven. Born in Germany, Elsa moved to the United States. She had a tendency toward wild relationships with the opposite sex. In fact, her whole life was one of extremes; she could not help but let chaos reign. Of course, such heavy drama—such a jump-off-the-pages storyline—is good fodder for fiction.

Stone, Irving.
The Agony and the Ecstasy. **1961.** NAL. paper. 776pp. ISBN 0-451-21323-8.

A classic biographical novel, still enthusiastically read, in many cases by readers who do not consider themselves particular fans of historical fiction—which testifies to the full-bodied reconstruction the book so engrossingly supplies of the conditions , crises, and triumphs that comprised the path to immortality taken by an important and complicated historical figure, Renaissance artist Michelangelo. This is a major factor in the novel's effectiveness and popularity—an understanding of the dramatic series of events that were so much part of everyone's lives in the Italy of that era (in Michelangelo's case, a tale of both spilled blood *and* spilled paint).

Vantrease, Brenda Rickman.

The Illuminator. **2005.** St. Martin's. 416pp. ISBN 0-312-33191-6.

The title refers to the protagonist's stock-in-trade—he illuminates books with exquisite, painstakingly rendered paintings. The time is the fourteenth century, the place is England, and this exquisitely detailed novel tells an atmospheric story of love and loyalty, politics and religion, within the feudal order of the day. The written word still fell within the domain of the privileged, but such a concept was at least in the process of being challenged.

Vreeland, Susan.

Girl in Hyacinth Blue. **1999.** MacMurray & Beck. 242pp. ISBN 1-878448-90-0; Penguin. paper. 256pp. ISBN 0-14-029628-X.

Vreeland creates a marvelous conceit through which to tell her involved and involving story—tracing the ownership over the centuries of a Vermeer painting. The plot is launched in the present day, when a professor reveals to a colleague his secret possession of a painting he attributes to the famous painter from Delft. Subsequently, the author ushers the reader back through layers of time, through the lives of the painting's owners, reflecting not only essential moments in their lives but also what the painting's beauty meant to them.

Alternate Lifestyles

Not everyone has led his or her life according to generally accepted norms. Here are characters who broke the mold and the rules—making for fascinating reading.

Greene, Harlan.

The German Officer's Boy. **2005.** University of Wisconsin/Terrace. 214pp. ISBN 0-299-20810-9.

In November 1938, a young Jewish man, Herschel Grynszpan, attacked the German embassy in Paris, which resulted in the retaliatory and dreadful *Kristallnacht* in Germany (a widespread attack, which occurred during the course of only one night, on Jewish-owned businesses). In this sensitive but also erotic treatment of this actual historical incident, Greene portrays the motive behind the boy's act not as Jewish patriotism but as revenge against his male lover, a diplomat in the embassy.

Hall, Sarah.

The Electric Michelangelo. **2005.** Perennial. paper. 368pp. ISBN 0-06-081724-0.

Ah, the artistic life: highly romantic—at least that is the popular conception of it. Well, this "artist," Cyril Parks by name, practices in the medium of scarring ink into the skin; in other words, he is a tattoo artist. His tale begins in the early twentieth century at his mother's seaside resort in England, and his vocation takes him to Coney Island in America. His adventures, rendered in roundabout, picaresque fashion, lead him not from light-filled garret studio or salon or exotic locale to draw and paint, but to and from much shadier places and encounters with an assortment of colorful characters, who are made more colorful by the body decoration Cyril provides them. It's the path he chose, and the reader accompanies him with eyes wide open.

Hugo, Victor.
 The Hunchback of Notre Dame. **1831.** Barnes & Noble Books. paper. 608pp. ISBN 1-5930-8047-6.

This classic of French (and world) literature relates the famous (and elaborately but rivetingly plotted) tragedy of Quasimodo, the physically imperfect bell ringer of Paris's Notre Dame cathedral. Chosen the Prince of Fools because of his extreme ugliness, Quasimodo, during the fête the Parisians conduct to celebrate the marriage of the king's daughter in 1482, comes to rescue the condemned gypsy dancer, Esmerelda. Oh, what a beautiful tale.

Jennings, Gary.
 Raptor. **1982.** Bantam. paper. 928pp. ISBN 0-553-56282-7.

Here Jennings does for the Roman Empire (or, more specifically, for the Gothic conquest of Rome) what he did for the Aztec empire his epic trilogy (annotated in chapter 1). He focuses chiefly on characters, both those rendered historically accurately and the product of his creative imagination, in this instance, quite an unusual hero, Thorn, a hermaphrodite who eventually comes to serve Theodoric, king of the Ostrogoths. Also as in his Aztec novels, Jennings uses this character as a device to depict the whole of the culture. This exploration of Thor's androgyny, his ability to act as both man and woman, has fascinating consequences set within bloody battles, graphic sex scenes, and other cultural aspects of the provincial byways of the Roman Empire.

Reed, Jeremy.
 Boy Caesar. **2004.** Peter Owen; dist. by Dufour. paper. 220pp. ISBN 0-7206-1193-8.

This sexually graphic novel shifts back and forth in time, from past to present and back again, and so on. The past is the reign of the third-century Roman emperor Heliogabalis, flamboyantly homosexual; and the present is contemporary London, where a young gay man writes his doctoral dissertation on the "swinging" boy-emperor, searching for his own identity as a gay man while conducting his research, and filling in the blanks in the emperor's conduct as a gay leader and its consequences.

Renault, Mary.
The Persian Boy. **1972.** Vintage. paper. 432pp. ISBN 0-394-75101-9.

Renault wrote a series of novels set in ancient Greece, and this emotionally effective one has endured as her most popular. The title refers to the male servant and lover of Alexander the Great, the beautiful slave boy and eunuch Bagoas. It is through Bagoas's sharp but ever-loving eyes that the reader witnesses the last years of the great Macedonian king's brief life, related in a flowing but precise and never overwrought prose style.

Truong, Monique.
The Book of Salt. **2003.** Houghton. 261pp. ISBN 0-618-30400-2; Mariner. paper. 272pp. ISBN 0-618-44688-5.

The creative premise of this novel is that the narrator, a gay Vietnamese man, tells about his life as cook for the famous expatriate couple Gertrude Stein and Alice B. Toklas in Paris between the world wars. His employers' literary life and his enjoyment of being an ancillary figure in it are counterpoised by his memories of being an outcast in his homeland (because of his sexual orientation) and his sense of being forever an exile—for it is not as easy for him to accommodate himself to permanent exile as it is for Stein and Toklas.

The Apple and the Apple Tree

Apples never fall far from the tree, nor does the tree ever cease casting its shadow over the fallen apples. Portraits of families and their tragic dysfunctions populate these novels.

Chang, Lan Samantha.
Inheritance. **2004.** Norton. 288pp. ISBN 0-393-05919-7.

Family betrayal that casts its dark shadow over succeeding generations is at the heart of this quietly but forcefully rendered first novel, which begins in China in 1931 with two sisters, one of whom undergoes an arranged marriage; the other sets off the generations-haunting betrayal.

Clarke, George Elliott.
George & Rue. **2005.** Carroll & Graf. 223pp. ISBN 0-7867-1620-7.

This first novel takes American readers into a setting, and a specific milieu within that setting, with which they will be unfamiliar: Nova Scotia, Canada, in the 1920s to 1940s, but specifically within the black community of that province. (The sizable black population is descended from black Americans who migrated northward during the Revolutionary War and early nineteenth century.) Two young black brothers are hanged for murder in 1949, and Clarke (a cousin of these real-life individuals) goes back in time to investigate the origins of their unlawful ways, finding the source in the terrible abuse the brothers and their mother suffered at the hands of the boys' father. Told in a bold, syncopated, highly poetic voice.

Gregory, Philippa.

The Other Boleyn Girl. **2001.** Touchstone. paper. 664pp. ISBN 0-7432-2744-1.

The Queen's Fool. **2004.** Touchstone. paper. 504pp. ISBN 0-7432-4607-1.

The Virgin's Lover. **2004.** Touchstone. 448pp. ISBN 0-7432-5615-8.

This trio about Tudor England is "history lite": an easily followed narrative without weighty literary devices. Gregory effectively captures the atmosphere of intrigue that marked the Tudor court. The first novel is about the rivalry between the two Boleyn sisters for the affection of Henry VIII; the second is about the life-and-possible-death struggle for the throne between the half-sisters Mary I and Elizabeth I; and the third features the drama of the early years of Elizabeth's glorious reign—she could never forget she was the Great Harry's daughter but also the daughter of the executed and reviled Anne Boleyn.

Haley, Alex.

Roots. **1974.** Dell. paper. 736pp. ISBN 0-440-17464-3.

This is the quintessential family saga, defining the genre; a seminal work, it began the trend toward the grand sweep through family history set within the larger picture of social and political history. Seven generations of a black family are followed, from an African village to the modern era, concluding with a writer, who is Haley himself. The entire history of slaveholding and repression of blacks is reflected in these vivid pages.

Settle, Mary Lee.

The Killing Ground. **1982.** University of South Carolina. paper. 260pp. ISBN 1-57003-118-5.

This concluding volume in Settle's compelling Beulah Quintet, following *The Scapegoat*, brings the story of the Virginia families she has been tracing from one generation to the next up to the present day. Hannah McKarkle is presented as the author of the previous Beulah novels; here she goes in search of her roots, and it is obvious that memory, family, and clans have been the overarching elements of her heritage.

Sprott, Duncan.

The Ptolemies. **2004.** Knopf. 496pp. ISBN 1-4000-4154-6.

A vivid novel that chronicles the 300-year dynasty of the Ptolemies, the Greek line of pharaohs of Egypt (which included the famous Cleopatra), founded by one of Alexander the Great's generals. Your average family next door? You have no idea—till you read this rich account of family dysfunction. You'd never turn your back on one of these fellows—or ladies.

Artful Mix: Combining the Real and the Fictional

Find in these novels an exceptionally fluid, compatible, and comfortable mixture of characters the authors have invented and some they borrowed from the true annals of history.

Barker, Pat.
Regeneration. **1991.** Plume. paper. 250pp. ISBN 0-452-27007-3.

Based on the work of the very real psychiatrist Dr. W. H. R. Rivers, who treated shell-shocked British soldiers during World War I, this absolutely riveting novel boasts, first and foremost, the author's exceptional fictional rendering of historical figures, and second, grippingly executed dialogue, which is essential conversation about pacifism in the face of complete mobilization for war and about getting over one's psychological wounds to be able to return to the front.

Finney, Patricia.
Unicorn's Blood. **1998.** Picador. paper. 384pp. ISBN 0-312-20039-0.

Queen Elizabeth I of England—her arresting personality and the politics of her significant reign—continues to fascinate and to be a popular subject of historical fiction. This particular novel is a sequel to the author's *Firedrake's Eye*; it, like its predecessor, is an exceptionally colorful depiction of the time through Finney's extremely clever plot. As a young woman, Princess Elizabeth kept a diary that is lost, and if it is found and falls into the wrong hands, it could have vast consequences for her regime. Real and fictitious characters co-populate this intriguing novel with comfort and ease.

George, Margaret.
Mary Called Magdalene. **2002.** Penguin. paper. 656pp. ISBN 0-14-200279-8.

George specializes in copiously researched and elaborately presented fictional biographies of significant historical figures, and here she moves into the biblical world for a would-be memoir by the enigmatic but compelling Mary Magdalene, about whom little information is certain. But George understands Mary well and establishes for her a fully detailed life, which in turn provides rich details about the time and place in which she lived and the people who inhabited her world.

Pynchon, Thomas.
Mason & Dixon. **1997.** Picador. paper. 784pp. ISBN 0-312-42320-9.

Pynchon has a reputation for being somewhat difficult to read, and this, his fifth, novel, will certainly challenge readers with not only its length but also its elaborate plot and difficult language. Here, the author depicts the lives of Charles Mason and Jeremiah Dixon, who surveyed the Pennsylvania–Maryland border, which became known as the Mason-Dixon Line, the boundary between North and South. A rich saga that explores the cultural and scientific issues of the mid-eighteenth century.

Shaara, Jeff.
Rise to Rebellion. **2001.** Ballantine. 512pp. ISBN 0-345-42753-X; Ballantine. paper. 512pp. ISBN 0-345-42754-8.

Shaara, who has written another novel about the Revolutionary War (see *The Glorious Cause*) as well as one about the Mexican–American War (*Gone for Soldiers*), casts his fictional net farther back in time in this novel, for a richly imagined, you-are-there chronicle of the growing colonial opposition to the British might-makes-right form of control. Such historical figures as Benjamin Franklin, George Washington, and John Adams are given flesh, blood, and breath, coming alive, as also are the fictional characters Shaara devises.

Stevenson, Jane.
The Winter Queen. **2002.** Houghton. 308pp. ISBN 0-618-14912-0; Mariner. paper. 336pp. ISBN 0-618-14912-0.

The first installment of a trilogy (followed by *The Shadow King* and *The Empress of the Last Days*) about politics, war, and diplomacy in seventeenth-century Europe has as its specific focus Elizabeth Stuart, sister of England's Charles I and called the "Winter Queen" of Bohemia. In Holland, where she resides, she falls in love with a totally fictitious character—Pelagius van Overmeer, a black ex-slave and African prince. The tenor of life in the Low Countries at that time is as authentically and carefully evoked as the frenetic political issues of the day are brought to vivid life—as are all the actual and real characters.

Strauss, Darin.
Chang and Eng. **2000.** Plume. paper. 336pp. ISBN 0-452-28109-1.

From Siam (not Thailand), born in 1811 on a houseboat, the conjoined twins Chang and Eng Bunker became international celebrities before they were 20 years old. They were a circus act, and eventually settled in the pre–Civil War South, marrying two sisters from North Carolina; between them they fathered 21 children! In an amazing feat of empathy, author Strauss enters into their story, fictionalizing it but retaining historically minded realism and, using his obvious talents as a novelist, humanizing the brothers and making them fully dimensional, credible characters brought out of the sensational pages of history and, importantly, rescued from freakishness.

Unlikely Heroes

These characters are not cut from the usual hero's cloth, but their lack of heroic adornments results in fascinating reading.

Bielski, Nella.
The Year Is '42. **2004.** Pantheon. 224pp. ISBN 0-375-42286-2.

The author is a contemporary Ukrainian novelist and playwright, and her latest novel finds its narrative footing in Paris and Kiev during a year when World War II rages on, seemingly unwinnable for the Germans. A sophisticated *Wehrmacht* officer stationed in occupied Paris finds life away from the front not so difficult, but then he falls under suspicion of Resistance leanings and is posted to the much more difficult Eastern Front, where his friendship with a physician provides both a physical (in the form of relief from a skin infection) and mental respite.

Doyle, Roddy.
A Star Called Henry. **1999.** Penguin. paper. 402pp. ISBN 0-14-303461-8.

With beautiful, stylistic flourishes, Irish fiction and screen writer Doyle profiles a young man who lived in the streets of Dublin from childhood. Smart, handsome, and clever, Henry is not to be kept down; despite his harsh early life, he participates in the 1916 Easter Rising and becomes a member of the IRA—and gains knowledge of the opposite sex as well.

Fast, Howard.
Spartacus. **1951.** M. E. Sharpe/North Castle. paper. 372pp. ISBN 1-56324-599-X.

Most people know this novel for its 1960 movie version (starring Kirk Douglas), but actually *reading* the novel is as much a vivid invitation to visit ancient Rome as the movie is. The overall setting is a slave revolt, and the protagonist is the leader of the rebellion, the historical figure called Spartacus. His experiences, as Fast reconstructs them, are a well-conceived representation of a significant segment of Roman society, and learning about Spartacus's life and character is quite involving.

Hays, Edward.
The Passionate Troubadour. **2004.** Forest of Peace. paper. 638pp. ISBN 0-939516-69-1.

A flesh-and-blood, vigorous St. Francis of Assisi, the famous saint who renounced earthly possessions for a life of poverty, emerges from this fictional biography; reconciling his inner split between ascetic spirituality and being a real human is the framework upon which this authentically detailed novel is based. St. Francis's road to holiness is fully dramatized, not presented as an empty, shallow, remote story inapplicable to most lives, which could have happened in the hands of a less-accomplished writer.

Keneally, Thomas.
Schindler's List. **1982.** Simon & Schuster. 400pp. ISBN 0-671-51688-4; Touchstone. paper. 528pp. ISBN 0-671-51171-8.

Translated by Steven Spielberg into a critically well-received movie, Australian Keneally's Booker Prize–winning novel presents a fictionalized version of the life and life-sustaining work of Oskar Schindler, a German industrialist who endeavored to save more than a thousand Jewish prisoners under the Third Reich. Schindler is stubborn and given to taking advantage of opportunities for his own sake, and his less-than-noble character traits are important ingredients of his unexpected role as savior.

Maria, Sandor.
Casanova in Balzano. **2004.** Knopf. 304pp. ISBN 0-375-41337-5; Vintage. paper. 304pp. ISBN 0-375-71296-8.

The (in)famous lover Casanova walks out of jail after a 16-month, Inquisition-sponsored stint, and heads to the South Tyrol town of Balzano, where he resumes his usual activities. With the intense psychological insight for which this late Hungarian writer is known, and in extremely fluid prose, Casanova's new predicament of the heart and body is beautifully drawn.

Millhauser, Steven.
Martin Dressler: The Tale of an American Dreamer. **1996.** Vintage. Paper. 304pp. ISBN 0-679-78127-7.

The novel's eponymous main character is an American type: his business career in turn-of-the-twentieth-century New York City is launched in young manhood by working in his father's cigar store; he has vision but he also, as the title indicates, walks with his head in the clouds. His rise to hotel magnate leads him to create increasingly extravagant establishments, which in his mind are complete worlds unto themselves, in Disney World–like fashion. But the inside of himself, his soul, is more difficult to fulfill. Happiness eludes him, despite his material success. An easy plot formula, to be sure, but Millhauser brings a particular insight to his main character, the searching type.

Olds, Bruce.
Bucking the Tiger. **2001.** Farrrar. 240pp. ISBN 0-374-11727-6; Picador. paper. 384pp. ISBN 0-312-42024-2.

The major feature of Olds's creative fictional biography of frontier dentist and folk hero Doc Holliday is the mixed format. The author, in making his protagonist a fully dimensional, convincing, authentic character (consumptive, passionate, addicted to gambling, but also a gentleman), makes use of poems, newspaper pieces, song lyrics, fictionalized first-person accounts, and even made-up correspondence.

Vidal, Gore.
Burr. **1973.** Vintage. paper. 430pp. ISBN 0-375-70873-1.

   Aaron Burr is one of the most controversial figures in American history: a Founding Father and vice president of the United States under Thomas Jefferson, but the murderer—in a duel in 1804—of the greatly esteemed Alexander Hamilton, and tried and acquitted for treason in 1807. Vidal, a vastly intelligent and learned fiction writer, allows the always-up-to-something Burr to tell his side of events in this understanding and understandable portrait.

Witness to Important Events

The characters are not exactly standing on the sidelines of history but are history's observers of consequential figures and happenings.

Alexander, Robert.
The Kitchen Boy. **2003.** Penguin. paper. 229pp. ISBN 0-14-200381-6.

   In this riveting, highly imaginative, and breathtaking interpretation of a tragic event in Russian history, the politically out-of-touch yet privately affectionate ex-Czar Nicholas and his consort, Empress Alexandra, who were executed with their children in 1918 by the Bolsheviks, are witnessed close up by someone with intimate access to the imperial family during their Siberian exile.

Bruce, Duncan A.
The Great Scot: A Novel of Robert the Bruce, Scotland's Legendary Warrior King. **2004.** St. Martin's/Truman Talley. 368pp. ISBN 0-312-32396-4.

   From the perspective of hindsight, a returned soldier who was the confidant of Scotland's great twelfth-century king, Robert the Bruce, relates events as he observed them, and depicts the king as he saw him during the Bruce's long and important reign, especially as an effective military leader (employing guerrilla warfare as opposed to more traditional confrontation), never short on bravery in the heat of battle.

Byrd, Max.
Jefferson. **1993.** Bantam. paper. 432pp. ISBN 0-553-37937-2.

   This fictionalized biography of the third American president is the first of the author's trilogy of historical novels about particularly interesting chief executives; its trilogy "mates" are *Jackson* and *Grant*. The "central intelligence" here, the narrator of events, is Jefferson's secretary while he is in

Paris as minister of the new American nation, who endeavors to fathom his boss's compulsiveness, particularly his captivation with the lovely Maria Cosway, wife of a British artist.

Fast, Howard.
April Morning. **1961.** Bantam. paper. 208pp. ISBN 0-553-27322-1.

The title of this classic historical novel, by the late (d. 2003) dean of American historical novelists (see also *Spartacus*), refers to the April morning (the nineteenth, to be exact) in the fateful year 1775, when the momentous movement called the Revolutionary War began at the Battles of Lexington and Concord in Massachusetts. The history-altering events are related by a 15-year-old farmer's son, who sees his father die from an English bullet, which compels him to enlist.

Hansen, Ron.
Hitler's Niece. **1999.** Perennial. paper. 320pp. ISBN 0-06-0932201.

Through the eyes of Hitler's half-sister's daughter, with whom the Führer had a close relationship (he was quite besotted with her, in fact), the stunning rise of and the perverse personality of one of history's most notorious dictators are charted and caught with both historical accuracy and, where needed (coming up with his version of the niece's death, details of which no one can be certain about), plausible imagination.

Nye, Robert.
The Late Mr. Shakespeare. **1999.** Penguin. paper. 416pp. ISBN 0-14-028952-6.

For this British writer's other novels based on the lives of real Elizabethan figures, see *Falstaff* and *The Voyage of the Destiny*. This particular novel is about the Bard of Avon, whose life is observed by a youth who is part of Shakespeare's acting troupe, and who now relates his story in old age. Ribald and extremely inventive, this is a deeply etched and resonant portrait of this great man and his equally great times.

Olafsson, Olaf.
Walking into the Night. **2003.** Pantheon. 272pp. ISBN 0-375-42254-4; Anchor. paper. 265pp. ISBN 0-4000-3480-9.

This Icelandic-born novelist (now resident in the United States) integrates real and fictional characters into a rich, dynamic, and psychologically astute novel focusing on the butler of the famous (and wealthy) newspaperman William Randolph Hearst, at home in the 1930s in San Simeon, his lofty perch above the California coast. The butler witnesses a parade of high-placed figures, and at the same time is haunted by thoughts about his past, about which no one in his present life knows anything.

Thomas, Chantal.
Farewell, My Queen. **2002.** Touchstone. paper. 233pp. ISBN 0-7432-6078-3.

Twenty years after the fact and in exile from the place in which the events occurred, Madame Agathe-Sidonie Laborde, whose court duty it was to read aloud to Queen Marie Antoinette, recalls the turning-point days of 1789, when the fractures in the ancient regime cracked wide open. How the Palace of Versailles operated under its elaborate system of court etiquette, its opulent decor and decorations, all awash with gossip and rumors, is brought indelibly to light.

From Here to There: The Story of Immigration

The story of the United States is the story of people coming from other lands to make a better life, but it is also the story of other colonized countries.

Allende, Isabel.
Daughter of Fortune. **1998.** Perennial. paper. 399pp. ISBN 0-06-019491-X.
Portrait in Sepia. **2001.** Perennial. paper. 304pp. ISBN 0-06-621161-1.

This pair of colorful novels follows the adventures of, as well as the adventures of, the *descendants* of, a woman named Eliza Summers, born and raised in prosperity in the English community in early-nineteenth-century Chile. Eliza travels to California in pursuit of her love—the California of the 1849 Gold Rush. She has entered a world of impropriety, brimming with newcomers from the East as well as Asia. *Portrait in Sepia*, the second of the duet of novels, sees Eliza's granddaughter, Aurora, carrying the story of her grandmother further, but this is more the story of Aurora's other grandmother, a formidable Chilean woman established on Nob Hill in San Francisco.

Erdrich, Louise.
The Master Butcher's Club. **2003.** HarperCollins. 480pp. ISBN 0-06-620977-3; Perennial. paper. 416pp. ISBN 0-06-093533-2.

One of the most distinguished and beloved contemporary American fiction writers here turns to North Dakota in the four decades after World War I for a warm, vibrant, plot and psychologically complex and completely riveting story of a German veteran of that war, who marries the widow of his best friend and sets out for America, carrying a suitcase of sausages and a set of butcher's knives. His adventures in the New World and a new culture involve romance and mystery and encompass readers completely in the hero's story.

Janoda, Jeff.
    Saga. **2005.** Academy Chicago. 353pp. ISBN 0-89733-532-5.

        Based on a thirteenth-century Icelandic saga written by an unknown author, this detail-rich novel is about the colonization of Iceland by Norwegian settlers. It opens a wide-angled view into the difficult agrarian lifestyle the colonizers faced. In this narrative the tribal and clan government is brought to light and made relevant to contemporary readers, who are immediately made to understand that the fundament of life was land:, who owned it and who wanted to take it away. Honor, too, was very much a component of everyday life, and these folks guarded it with their lives.

Ozick, Cynthia.
    Heir to the Glimmering World. **2004.** Houghton. 310pp. ISBN 0-618-47049-2.

        In a novel that could be described as "high brow" for its extremely literary artistry, Ozick nonetheless achieves remarkable psychological subtlety and shading as she limns the lives of a very idiosyncratic German-Jewish family of exiles newly resident in a remote corner of the Bronx in the mid-1930s. Vastly intelligent, absorbingly riveting, and gorgeously written, this is a novel about aliens in a strange land, wanderers from a secure previous life, fugitives from pasts they cannot reconcile with the difficult present.

Settle, Mary Lee.
    O Beulah Land. **1956.** University of South Carolina. paper. 368pp. ISBN 1-57003-115-0.

        The second volume in Settle's acclaimed <u>Beulah Quintet</u> (following *Prisons*) is set in Virginia between 1754 and 1774 and depicts, in the author's trademark vivid but never mannered prose, the defeat of British general Braddock at the hands of the French, as well as introducing the English and Scottish families that came over to settle the region and whose descendants the author will track in subsequent volumes in the quintet. Her theme of inherent class consciousness and distinctions is shown even in lower-class frontier society.

Tan, Amy.
    The Bonesetter's Daughter. **2001.** Ballantine. paper. 416pp. ISBN 0-80-441498-6.

        The fourth novel by the author of the ever-popular *The Joy Luck Club* (see below) also locates its heart in the relationship between a Chinese-born immigrant mother and her American-born daughter. Ruth is a writer living in San Francisco in the present day, and, in a situation typical of a Tan novel, she knows little about her mother's past or her mother's real, true self. Her mother has been diagnosed with Alzheimer's, and two packets of Chinese calligraphy, written by her mother, fall into Ruth's hands; a hired translator deciphers them for her. Ruth now learns about her mother's past, and with that, the major part of the novel is given over to a graphic, poignant visit to a remote region of China in the 1920s. Again, as do previous Tan novels, this one operates bilaterally, depicting both the rustic conditions of China in the first half of the twentieth century and the conflicts between immigrants from that land and their American-born children.

Tan, Amy.
The Joy Luck Club. **1989.** Ballantine. paper. 352pp. ISBN 0-8041-9896-9.

Tan's first novel was not only a popular success but also greatly contributed to the rise of fictional immigration narratives about Asians coming to the United States. This novel follows, with admirably penetrating historical, cultural, and psychological detail, four Chinese women who fled the post–World War II chaos of the conflict between the Communists and Nationalists and came to San Francisco. For decades the four women, who had been friends, gathered each week to play mahjong and to tell their life stories. When one club member dies, her daughter is asked to take her place. Tan's compelling tapestry of personal stories includes women sacrificing their baby girls, brutal husbands, and refugee marches. Into this poignant mix are added the stories of the daughters of all the club members, the result being a complex tale of mother–daughter relations and the second generation immigrant's need to honor her heritage but at the same time be an American.

Tan, Amy.
The Kitchen God's Wife. **1991.** Ballantine. paper. 544pp. ISBN 0-8041-9897-7.

Tan's second novel borrows from its predecessor and is continued in its successor, using the immigrant mother, first-generation American daughter storytelling device. That cultural attitudes toward women left much to be desired in old China, at least when cast against the contemporary world's more enlightened views, is a concept that won't surprise most fiction readers. The story told here—a childhood starved of positive emotion and nurturing (her mother abandons her), then a dreadful arranged marriage—confirms that such treatment existed. But Winnie survives her trials in civil war–rent China in the 1940s, and she finds her own courage, sustained by women friends and her second husband. She divulges the secrets of her past to her American-born but distant daughter (who carries secrets of her own).

Tremain, Rose.
The Colour. **2003.** Farrar. 352pp. ISBN 0-374-12605-4; Picador. paper. 400pp. ISBN 0-312-42310-1.

The British author of the evocative *Restoration* here turns to a historical episode with which few Americans will be familiar: the nineteenth-century New Zealand gold rush. Immigrant life during those inherently tumultuous and competitive times is made vivid and unforgettable through an abundance of authentic detail about the lives of an English couple, whose destinies are at the mercy of gold—the "colour" of the novel's title.

Living Large

They do things on a grander scale than you and I . . . .

Bell, Madison Smartt.
   The Stone That the Builder Refused. **2004.** Pantheon. 768pp. ISBN 0-375-42282-X.

   This vibrant novel concludes Bell's magnificently executed trilogy about the late-nineteenth-century revolution to free Haiti from French rule, the world's only successful slave revolt, led by the full-bodied Toussaint Louverture. The preceding volumes are *All Soul's Rising* and *The Master of the Crossroads.* The final battles with French forces are rendered as dramatically as the color by which, and depth to which, the author creates all characters, primary and secondary—but *primarily* Louverture himself: brilliant tactician, astute in politics, yet illusory and contradictory, and looming over Caribbean history for his outstanding achievement of independence.

Bordihn, Michael.
   The Falcon of Palermo. **2005.** Grove/Atlantic. paper. 432pp. ISBN 0-87113-880-8.

   The great Holy Roman Emperor Frederick II, who was in real life a powerful, magnetic personality, here in fictional form achieves his true, full dimensions as the central character in a revealing narrative based chiefly on true events. Acquainted at an early age with the Muslim quarter of Palermo, Frederick shows a sensitivity to that culture during his reign as king of Sicily. His ascent to the throne of the Holy Roman Empire introduces him to a host of different "management" problems, which he faces head on.

Byrd, Max.
   Jackson. **1997.** Bantam. paper. 432pp. ISBN 0-553-37935-6.

   Andrew Jackson was certainly not a refined individual; he was an angry, illiterate frontiersman. But he defeated the British at the Battle of New Orleans in the War of 1812, became a legend, and then became the seventh president of the United States. His firm belief in democracy for the masses brought about its own kind of political revolution once he was in the White House. Byrd has a strong reputation for good fictional biographies of presidents, in which all sides of the generally contradictory personalities he has chosen to write about come to light by way of different perspectives from people who surrounded them, and this sequel to *Jefferson* and *Grant* is a rich and revealing reading experience.

Dietrich, William.
The Scourge of God. **2005.** HarperCollins. 352pp. ISBN 0-06-073499-X.

The novel's title refers to Attila the Hun, who was feared by Roman citizens in the mid-fifth century; he was a warrior and leader of men with skill and force. He sought to conquer both the eastern and western halves of the Roman Empire, to that end destroying everything in his path. The author focuses on a small handful of fictitious characters, including a young Roman woman taken hostage by the Huns, all to add a human face to these dark days of battles and executions, but it is mighty Attila who looms over the narrative as his shadow loomed over Rome.

García Márquez, Gabriel.
The General in His Labyrinth. **1990.** Penguin. paper. 285pp. ISBN 0-14-014859-8).

Splendid, elegant, beautifully honed prose is what readers expect from this internationally beloved Colombian novelist, winner of the Nobel Prize. García Márquez's tough yet lovely language serves him well in this multifaceted portrait of the great South American liberator, Simon de Bolivar, whose memory in South America remains touched with the divine but who is seen here as a magnificent but still human figure.

McCullough, Colleen.
Caesar. **1997.** Avon. paper. 910pp. ISBN 0-06-051085-4.

In this volume in McCullough's Masters of Rome series, she tackles the greatest Roman of them all. Caesar was both hero and tyrant, adored and despised, and the author lets his large life and oversized personality reflect the tumult of the times. She is as adept at describing military matters as she is at establishing the complexities of her major character, in all his brilliance and ambitiousness.

Nye, Robert.
Falstaff. **2001.** Arcade. paper. 464pp. ISBN 1-55970-649-X.

A British novelist known for his fictionalized reconstruction of real Elizabethan figures (see also *The Voyage of the Destiny* and *The Late Mr. Shakespeare*), in this novel, which won the prestigious Hawthornden and Guardian fiction prizes, Nye brings to life a character who was already quite lively: Falstaff, one of Shakespeare's most memorable characters, who was based on an actual person. In the form of a memoir written by Falstaff, this novel is bawdy entertainment.

Machiavellian Men—and Women

They get what they want, which is political power, whatever it costs.

Iggulden, Conn.
Emperor: Gates of Rome. **2003.** Dell. paper. 480pp. ISBN 0-440-24094-8.
Emperor: The Death of Kings. **2004.** Dell. paper. 460pp. ISBN 0-440-24095-6.
Emperor: The Field of Swords. **2005.** Delacorte. 407pp. ISBN 0-385-33663-2.
    Three titles in the author's projected four-volume biographical novel about Julius Caesar, with special focus on his rise to power, are completed. The authentically, lusciously detailed tale ranges from Caesar's boyhood as a patrician well connected to the seat of Roman power, through his early military exploits, to his British campaign. This large, elaborate portrait of a man of ambition is edifyingly supported by the author's exploration of the functioning of the Roman state and the importance of the expansion of its boundaries, to the benefit of its leaders.

Martínez, Tomás Eloy.
The Peron Novel. **1988.** Random. paper. 435pp. ISBN 0-679-76801-7.
    This prequel to the author's absorbing *Santa Evita* (see below), related from different perspectives, is an intriguingly fashioned portrait of Argentine dictator General Juan Perón. The novel begins with Perón's return to Argentina from exile in Spain in 1973, and in mixed format—including newspaper reports and interviews—the rise of a charismatic man is recollected and his sinking into political ineffectiveness is witnessed.

Martínez, Tomás Eloy.
Santa Evita. **1996.** Random. paper. 384pp. ISBN 0-679-76814-9.
    Eva Perón, the small-potatoes actress who became the wife of and linchpin of the regime of Argentine dictator Juan Perón, continues to exert her controversial spell, even long after her death by cancer in 1952. The treatment of her embalmed corpse, which immediately gained the status of a sacred relic, is an almost unbelievable story of possession and manipulation, as Argentine politics shifted this way and that in the post-Perónist years. This talented Argentine novelist tells the story of Evita's "life after death," her mythological place in the Argentine historical consciousness, very well. This is a sequel to the author's *The Perón Novel* (see above).

Maxwell, Robin.
The Secret Diary of Anne Boleyn. **1997.** Touchstone. paper. 288pp. ISBN 0-684-84969-0.
The Queen's Bastard. **1999.** Touchstone. paper. 448pp. ISBN 0-684-85760-X.

Virgin: Prelude to the Throne. **2001.** Touchstone. paper. 256pp. ISBN 0-7432-0485-9.

The Wild Irish: A Novel of Elizabeth I and the Pirate O'Malley. **2003.** Perennial. paper. 400pp. ISBN 0-06-009143-6.

What is it about the Tudor era in English history, especially the life and reign of Elizabeth I, that makes it such rich—and perennially popular—fodder for historical novelists? The answer can be found in the lush pages of this sequence of novels—the answer being the intriguing character of Elizabeth herself. These novels follow Elizabeth Tudor from her perilous teenage years, when she was coming of age as a woman and princess; to her early years as queen, discovering, so Maxwell has it, a diary brimming with revelations that was kept by her executed mother, Queen Anne Boleyn; to the relationship between Queen Elizabeth and the Earl of Leicester, from which, again as Maxwell has imaginatively has it, springs a bastard son; to her problems with an Irish rebellion.

Min, Anchee.
Becoming Madame Mao. **2000.** Morrow. paper. 330pp. ISBN 0-618-12700-3.

The author of the well-received *Empress Orchid,* a novelization of the fascinating early life of the controversial Dowager Empress who presided over the final years of the Chinese imperial regime, reconstructs, again in fictional form but with the same historical accuracy, understanding, and even empathy, the life of another important and controversial woman highly placed in Chinese affairs. The wife of Mao Zedong (Jiang Qing) has gone down in history as the instigator of the Cultural Revolution, one of the many blights on twentieth-century Chinese history. Min here does not take the popular image of Madame Mao as gospel truth, preferring her own nuanced interpretation of the woman: driven by passion but suffering from no traces of self-doubt, and even cruel and pathologically needy.

Tuck, Lily.
The News from Paraguay. **2004.** HarperCollins. 272pp. ISBN 0-06-620944-7; HarperCollins. paper. 272pp. ISBN 0-06-093486-7.

The author bases this atmospheric novel, which won the National Book Award, on two historical figures: the nineteenth-century Paraguayan dictator Francisco Solano López and his Irish-born mistress, Ella Lynch. The havoc wreaked upon his country by "Franco's" brutal administration, including a disastrous war with Brazil and Argentina, is supported by the much-privileged Ella. A sad but well-told story, with convincingly achieved characterizations.

Vargas Llosa, Mario.
The Feast of the Goat. **2001.** Farrar. 416pp. ISBN 0-374-15467-7; Picador. paper. 400pp. ISBN 0-312-42027-7.

This is at once a raw, bloody, sensuous, and gorgeously written fictional (but highly accurate in its lush historical detail) depiction of death of the infamous Dominican Republic strongman Rafael ("the Goat") Trujillo. The author, a Peruvian novelist recognized the world over as a major figure in international literature, focuses on Trujillo's assassination in 1961 to arrive at a deeply understood, well-shaded portrait of a tyrant and the traits of his particular tyranny.

I'm in This Alone

People do what they have to do, and do it for and by themselves.

Byatt, A. S.
Babel Tower. **1996.** Vintage. paper. 640pp. ISBN 0-679-7380-8.

This novel, the third installment in the author's quartet about English life in the middle years of the twentieth century, brings the story up to the 1960s—barely falling into the definition of "historical fiction," but it really is just that. Byatt chronicles the times by focusing on Frederica, the major character found in the previous two novels in the sequence, *The Virgin in the Garden* and *Still Life*. The intellectual Frederica is a complex character in this novel with a complicated structure; in summary, Frederica, by necessity of her personality and needs, flees country-estate life and plunges head first into the London arts scene.

Gaines, Ernest.
A Lesson Before Dying. **1993.** Vintage. paper. 256pp. ISBN 0-375-70270-9.

Gaines is best known for the highly esteemed novel *The Autobiography of Miss Jane Pittman*. *A Lesson before Dying* is an extremely moving novel as well. Winner of the National Book Critics' Circle Award for Fiction, it is set in a small Cajun community in Louisiana in the late 1940s and is a searing portrayal of friendship between a young black man on death row and a black schoolteacher who visits him while he is in prison. This mutual educational process becomes an amazing path of self-discovery for both of them. ("You're not a boy. You're a man," the teacher tells him.)

Kantor, MacKinlay.
Long Remember. **1934.** Forge. paper. 376pp. ISBN 0-312-87520-7.

Readers will remember the language, brimming with stunning imagery, long after their initial encounter with this psychologically and descriptively rich first novel about the Battle of Gettysburg in the American Civil War. But it is the major character they will ultimately, resonantly, and lastingly recall: a young man, local to the Pennsylvania community that played "host" to one of the most consequential battles of the war, who must abandon his pacifist principles in the face of the awfulness transpiring around him.

Morrison, Toni.
Beloved. **1987.** Vintage. paper. 352pp. ISBN 1-4000-3341-1.

Is this novel this Nobel laureate's masterpiece? Probably not (most readers would site *Song of Solomon*, 1977, for that distinction). But certainly *Beloved* has left a lasting impression on the international reading public (aided by its continued resonance in the public consciousness through the movie version and being an Oprah book club selection). It is a significant and heartbreaking rendering of the vicissitudes of slavery. The setting is Ohio in the post–Civil War period. Sethe, the main character, was born a slave and escaped north to freedom, but several years later is still imprisoned by her memories, primarily of her unnamed baby, whose gravestone is marked simply "Beloved." She had murdered the little girl to avoid recapture. Borne on Morrison's trademark lyrical prose, this novel is a particularly searing indictment of the viciousness of slavery.

Phillips, Caryl.
Higher Ground: A Novel in Three Parts. **1989.** Vintage. paper. 224pp. ISBN 0-679-76376-7.

The three novellas gathered here act so well in concert that the book lives up to the author's insistence that it be regarded as a novel. The first section concerns the survival of an African man in the slave trade, who learns the language of the white traders; the second part is letters written by a black man in a Southern prison in the 1960s; and the third is about a woman in London who was separated from her Polish Jewish family during World War II. The connection between the three parts is how the author cuts to the quick of alienation, isolation, and despair, while making sure to impart the humanity of the characters.

Riviere, William.
Kate Caterina. **2002.** Grove/Atlantic. 384pp. ISBN 0-87113-839-5; Grove/Atlantic. paper. 365pp. ISBN 0-8021-3973-6.

An effective, dramatic, and poignant depiction of one individual's torn sensibilities and loyalties as the country of her birth and the country she has adopted as her homeland fall into war. An Englishwoman marries an Italian physician just prior to the outbreak of World War II, and she has just begun establishing herself in a new culture when suddenly she is an alien in an alien land.

Saramago, José.
The Gospel According to Jesus Christ. **1994.** Harvest. paper. 396pp. ISBN 0-15-600141-1.

This Portuguese Nobel prize winner habitually composes cerebral yet exciting novels, often with a historical setting, and this novel is by no means an exception to his custom. In this case, Saramago makes a foray into biblical fiction with a biographical novel about Jesus. Saramago's depiction of his main character as both Son of God and an all-too-human being (surrendering to the ways of the flesh) is a highly imaginative re-creation of both Jesus's psychology and the earthly environment in which his life was played out.

Rebels with a Cause

They offer resistance to the society around them, on a grand national scale or even on a small personal scale, all for good reasons.

Banks, Russell.
Cloudsplitter. **1998.** Perennial. paper. 768pp. ISBN 0-06-0930861-1.
> The narrator of this highly provocative novel is Owen Brown, son of fanatic abolitionist John Brown, executed in 1859 for his raid on the arsenal at Harpers Ferry, Virginia. Despite its length, this is a much more direct and immediate fictional treatment of the subject than Bruce Olds's highly impressionistic *Raising Holy Hell* (see below). The writing style is impressive and very much in keeping with the more formal writing of the times. John Brown the strange individual, and what he did, will haunt the reader nearly as much as the man and his actions haunt his son.

Bell, Madison Smartt.
Master of the Crossroads. **2000.** Vintage. paper. 752pp. ISBN 1-4000-7838-5.
> The second installment in Bell's magnificently researched and executed trilogy about the Haitian slave revolt in the 1790s, led by the charismatic Toussaint Louverture, follows *All Souls' Rising* and precedes *The Stone That the Builder Refused*. This middle volume takes readers deeply into the campaign against the French forces, with particular emphasis on the excellent tactician and smart politician that the great liberator was.

Cornwell, Bernard.
Rebel. **1993.** Perennial. paper. 416pp. ISBN 0-06-093461-1.
> This volume inaugurated Cornwell's popular (but are any of his novels-in-series *not* popular?) Starbuck Chronicles, featuring the exploits and escapades of Civil War soldier Nathaniel Starbuck. This first entry introduces our hero, a Northern preacher's son who, when the war breaks out, is caught in the South and makes the decision to fight for the Confederacy. Battle scenes are rendered with great action and colorful detail, and Starbuck demonstrates well-drawn heroic traits.

Galloway, Janice.
Clara. **2003.** Simon & Schuster. paper. 448pp. ISBN 0-7432-3853-2.
> Clara Wieck Schumann, a famous nineteenth-century pianist in her own right, is nevertheless best remembered today as the wife of her more

famous husband, composer Robert Schumann. In this exquisitely written novel, the reader finds a remarkable and strong woman who opposed her domineering father to marry Schumann, who was beset by troublesome mental problems.

Olds, Bruce.
Raising Holy Hell. **1995.** Picador. paper. 352pp. ISBN 0-312-42093-5.

An accomplished—even astonishing in conception and effectiveness—first novel that in collage format (including quotations, newspaper articles, and interviews) imparts an indelible picture of the infamous abolitionist John Brown, best known for his attempted seizure of the armory at Harpers Ferry, Virginia. A fanatical personality, he is portrayed here in this provocative novel in all his disturbing dimensions. (See also *Cloudsplitter*, by Russell Banks, another novel about John Brown, that is much less impressionistic than this one.)

Ricci, Nino.
Testament. **2003.** Mariner. paper. 464pp. ISBN 0-618-44667-2.

This stunning, beautiful fictional account of the life led on Earth by Jesus is provocatively accomplished by relating his story from the perspectives of four individuals acquainted with him: Judas, who here, for Ricci's purposes, is a freedom fighter against Roman rule; Mary Magdalene, a disciple; Mary, Jesus's mother; and a fictitious shepherd, witness to Jesus's final days. Jesus is essentially made human here, with all the accouterments of human nature.

Vargas Llosa, Mario.
The War of the End of the World. **1981.** Penguin. paper. 576pp. ISBN 0-14-026260-1.

The great Peruvian writer supplies another masterwork in this breathtaking, gut-wrenching novel about an insurrection led by a messianic figure against the established order in the backwoods of late-nineteenth-century Brazil. Onto this vast canvas, at once brutally and beautifully wrought, Vargas Llosa casts an elaborate picture of the inherent conflict between social and political change on the one hand and the resistance to it on the other hand.

Brilliant Facsimile

These are fictional biographies of historical figures that read like the real thing.

Balint, Christine.

Ophelia's Fan. **2004.** Norton. 352pp. ISBN 0-393-05925-1; Norton. paper. 320pp. ISBN 0-393-05925-1.

Nineteenth-century Irish actress Harriet Smithson, a historical figure, serves as the protagonist in this richly appointed biographical novel. Harriet was born of itinerant players and became a hit on the London stage; paralleling Harriet's stage roles and the drama of her off-stage life results in not only an interesting character brought back to life but also the context in which she existed: the thrilling world of the theater in the early nineteenth century.

Byrd, Max.

Grant. **2000.** Bantam. paper. 368pp. ISBN 0-553-38018-4.

Grant was a heroic general in the Civil War who made a dismal U.S. president, but Byrd's intention in this, the third installment of his trilogy of fictional biographies of American presidents, including *Jefferson* and *Jackson*, is to reconstruct Grant's post-presidency, as he attempted to win a third term as president, experienced financial collapse, and lost a struggle with cancer, events that are related from the perspective of a veteran of the war who is now a newspaper reporter. As rich in historical detail and vivid psychological expression as Byrd's other two novels.

Haase, Hella.

In a Dark Wood Wandering. **1949.** Academy Chicago. paper. 594pp. ISBN 0-89-733356-X.

A lengthy but never tiresome fictionalized biography of Charles d'Orleans (1394–1465), nephew of French King Charles VI and cousin of the dauphin for whom Joan of Arc took a fateful stand, but most important, a great poet. The author is Dutch, and the novel was originally published in her native country; its appearance in English enabled wider advertising of its merits, which are a sharp understanding of the central character, a meticulous historical reconstruction of politics and military affairs during the Hundred Years War, and a carefully honed writing style.

Nye, Robert.

The Voyage of the **Destiny.** **2003.** Arcade. paper. 400pp. ISBN 1-55970-695-3.

From a veteran writer of historical novels, this is a fictionalized version of the life of the great Elizabethan adventurer, Sir Walter Raleigh. Recently released from the Tower of London by the tricky King James I, Raleigh relates his present escapades (searching in South America for gold for the crown) and recalls past ones; the total picture is a full-bodied portrait of a flawed but multidimensional figure.

Steinbeck, John.
Cup of Gold. **1929.** Penguin. paper. 238pp. ISBN 0-14-018743-X.

Steinbeck is so readily associated with fictional accounts of lettuce farmers of California's Central Valley that it is easy to forget that this, his first, novel is about "A Life of Henry Morgan, Buccaneer, with Occasional References to History." This is a vivid narrative based on the life of the (in)famous pirate of the Caribbean, with particular light shed on one exploit: sacking Panama City and making off with a married woman.

Stone, Irving.
Lust for Life. **1934.** Plume. paper. 489pp. ISBN 0-452-26249-6.

A master of the biographical novel reconstructs the life of famous Dutch painter Vincent van Gogh. Stone's novel amounts to an education for the curious reader interested in the events of Van Gogh's life, for general readers who know very little about his personal story, as well as a good psychological fathoming of his nature. From the very beginning of the novel, we see a person of extreme behavior, haunted by his thoughts.

Vidal, Gore.
Lincoln. **1984.** Vintage. paper. 672pp. ISBN 0-375-70876-6.

Distinguished man-of-letters Vidal, in his capacity as historical novelist, for which he enjoys a widespread reputation, has done no better than this fictionalized biography of the sixteenth president of the United States. Lincoln is an icon of the highest degree, and he is far from being reduced in stature here, his image far from wounded. In this monumental book he emerges with humility and ambiguity; in other words, with all the dimensions of a true human being.

The Darker Side of Human Nature

Nobody is perfect, of course—a situation that makes for delicious reading.

Braver, Adam.
Mr. Lincoln's Wars: A Novel in Thirteen Stories. **2003.** Avon. 320pp. ISBN 0-06-008118-X; Perennial. paper. 320pp. ISBN 0-06-008119-8.

An unusual and ultimately compelling fictional treatment of the life, times, and public and personal problems of the sixteenth president, this is a collection of short stories that, functioning as discrete units but at the same time as "cooperative" chapters, add up to a novel. Braver looks into the "head" of Lincoln, finding the darkness but also the resilience there as leader of a broken nation, father of children who have predeceased him, and husband of a difficult wife.

Eisner, Michael Alexander.
The Crusader. **2001.** Anchor. paper. 320pp. ISBN 0-385-72141-2.

The Crusades were a period, time, and series of incidents that practically shout adventure, military exploits, exotic locales, and intense relationships of the heart. The very workable conceit of this bold delving into all the color and cruelty of the Crusades is that a Spanish knight just back from fighting in the Holy Land in the last half of the thirteenth century dictates his story to be transcribed by his friend, a Cistercian monk with some darker aspects to his character. The knight has rather gone off the deep end from his horrendous experiences, and his father has offered a reward for his recovery, which the monk hopes to cash in on. An electric tale of rape, castration, torture, demonic possession, flaming passion, and, above all, catastrophic events caused by religious fervor. Hardly the story of glorious banner waving most people think of when they think of the Crusades.

Golding, William.
The Spire. **1964.** Harvest. paper. 228pp. ISBN 0-15-602782-8.

A staggeringly effective novel set in medieval England, about the ill-conceived construction of a cathedral spire (at Salisbury, one surmises), the whole process and the cathedral community distinctly and precisely rendered. But this project—obsession—of the dean of the cathedral, which is to be a tribute to the glory of God, becomes disastrously drenched in the effects of the eternal struggle between good and evil and between human will and the inexorable forces of nature.

Hambly, Barbara.
The Emancipator's Wife. **2005.** Bantam. 624pp. ISBN 0-553-80301-8.

One of the most famous—or infamous—first ladies in American history, but certainly one of the most interesting as well, Mary Todd Lincoln is portrayed with great understanding and compassion in this compelling fictional account. We see an individual assailed by spells, visions, and hysteria, beginning in her childhood. Mental balance was difficult for her to maintain after the death of three of the Lincolns' four sons, and especially following the assassination of her husband.

Lagerkvist, Pär.
Barabbas. **1951.** Vintage. paper. 160pp. ISBN 0-679-72544-X.

Lagerkvist, a Swede, won the Nobel Prize for Literature in 1951, which brought him a certain international fame—but not as much as he deserves, given the stirring power of his themes, rendered in exquisite prose, as demonstrated in this unforgettable novel about the murderer who was pardoned instead of Jesus, by public acclaim. The novel depicts Barabbas's post-reprieve spiritual torment.

Mallon, Thomas.
Henry and Clara. **1994.** Picador. paper. 368pp. ISBN 0-312-13508-4.

> Mallon's novel is a wonderfully imagined embroidery of the two basic facts known about two historically insignificant but nevertheless personally interesting witnesses to a vastly consequential event. Major Henry Rathbone and Clara Harris, an engaged couple, were guests of the first couple in the presidential box at Ford's Theatre the night Lincoln was shot. But Mallon found more to them than that; he tells a tale of murder and madness in the wake of the nationally and personally devastating event they so closely observed.

Phillips, Max.
The Artist's Wife. **2001.** Welcome Rain. paper. 256pp. ISBN 1-56649-273-4.

> Falling within the subgenre of historical fiction called fictional autobiography, this novel is the first-person recollection—told from the grave—of Alma Mahler (1877–1964), daughter of a famous landscape painter and darling of turn-of-the-century Vienna. She married famous composer Gustav Mahler and then well-known architect Walter Gropius and had many liaisons, all the while exhibiting little kindness beneath her lovely exterior.

Wilson, Jonathan.
A Palestine Affair. **2003.** Pantheon. 272pp. ISBN 0-375-42209-9; Anchor. paper. 257pp. ISBN 1-4000-3122-2.

> The time is 1924 and the place is British-controlled Palestine. The plot centers on three characters—a man and his wife and the police officer investigating a murder the couple witnessed—who come to the region from England and the United States to turn their backs on past grief caused by events in the recent world war, but find themselves confronting the same issues—identity and loss and one's personal concept of life's meaning—in a different form and place.

History's Forgotten Heroes

Outwardly small people can inwardly have great courage and force of personality.

Brink, Andre.
The Other Side of Silence. **2003.** Harvest. paper. 320pp. ISBN 0-15-602964-2.

> Hanna X flees torment in a German orphanage to Africa, only to find more brutalization in the German colonies there. But revenge is now hers, and she leads a vigilante group of victims of colonization against the very might of the German Empire itself at the turn of the twentieth century.

Buck, Pearl.

The Good Earth. **1931.** Washington Square. paper. 368pp. ISBN 0-671-03577-9.

This simple but definitely not simplistic novel has been charming readers since its publication. One of the many novels by the first American woman to win the Nobel Prize for Literature (in 1938), *The Good Earth* has attained classic status because of its perennial timeliness and the universality of its thematic underpinnings: the grace of common folk and the inexorable cycle of birth and death, played out in this case on a farm in China in the early years of the twentieth century. The experiences with his wives and children and land of a quietly noble farmer are far removed from the elaborate structures and strictures of the imperial court in Peking.

Charlesworth, Monique.

The Children's War. **2004.** Knopf. 384pp. ISBN 1-4000-4009-4.

Two European children from quite different backgrounds (one a German of mixed Jewish-Christian parentage, the other the son of a wealthy German family heavily tied to the Nazi Party) are the focus of this complex and engaging novel about, on one level, personal safety during World War II in the face of the Reich's institutionalized anti-Semitism and later Allied destruction. On a more metaphysical level, it is about salvation from both physical danger as well as political and financial insularity. In other words, it is about two children having to grow up—and doing so successfully.

Chase-Riboud, Barbara.

Hottentot Venus. **2003.** Doubleday. paper. 352pp. ISBN 0-385-50856-5.

Pulitzer Prize winner Chase-Ribaud relates in deeply humanizing terms the life story of a female member of the Khoe Khoe (Hottentot) tribe of South Africa. Sarah Baartman is a historical person who lived in the Dutch colonies of the early nineteenth century, and the author spins around the historical evidence a detailed and convincing interpretation of this victim of racism, who became a freak in a sideshow in Europe.

O'Brien, Patricia.

The Glory Cloak. **2004.** Touchstone. paper. 368pp. ISBN 0-7432-5750-2.

The backdrop of this dramatic, swiftly moving story of three female friends is the horrors of the Civil War, which alters the women's lives and perceptions forever. The fictitious character Susan Gray, who is displaced by the war, goes to live with her uncle and cousin, the latter the real-life Louisa May Alcott, future author of *Little Women.* They grow very close and eventually proceed to Washington, D.C., to do volunteer nursing. There they meet another actual historical figure, nurse Clara Barton. Friendship and nineteenth-century women's roles are immaculately analyzed.

Park, Jacqueline.
   The Secret Book of Grazia Dei Rossi. **1997.** Simon & Schuster. 576pp. ISBN
   0-684-84840-6.

      Renaissance Italy is certainly a fertile ground for fictional exploration,
and Park exquisitely mines that place and time (the sixteenth century) in this
purported secret memoir penned by one Grazia Dei Rossi, member of a
prominent Jewish family but the lover of a Christian knight and private secretary to the famous political figure Isabella d'Este. The secret book is her legacy to her son, confiding in him her life's paths, led by heart and mind. How
religious differences, and the resulting persecution, affected even the highly
placed in society behind the splendor of the Italian Renaissance is
dramatically rendered.

Walker, Margaret.
   Jubilee. **1966.** Mariner. paper. 512pp. ISBN 0-395-92495-2.

      Since its appearance in the heyday of 1960s black publishing, this
moving novel has established a firm and lasting reputation among readers
of all genders, races, and generations. It is based on a real person—the author's ancestor—who was born the daughter of a white plantation owner
and a black slave. She is smart and strong, and her story of adversity and
triumph re-creates with assured detail the treatment of blacks in the antebellum and Reconstruction American South.

Chapter 3

Story

When all is said and done, most people read fiction to be told a good story. In that way, fiction readers are forever children, taking great pleasure from sitting cross-legged on the floor at the knees of an adult who is talented in the finer points of reading a book aloud and dramatizing it to mesmerizing effect. "Story" is one of the chief appeal factors of novels in general and historical novels in particular. A storyline that embraces readers—grabbing them and leading them (with their full cooperation) along a path of adventure with exciting twists and turns, or even down a road very familiar to them (such as domestic pleasures and travails), with which they can easily identify—is what many readers insist upon first and foremost in their fiction reading. Authorial emphasis on, for example, slow and deliberate character development, or a particularly polished writing style, is of secondary interest to readers who turn to fiction—and that most definitely includes historical fiction—to be told a good story.

Such readers, by the very fact of their turning to historical fiction, naturally have an interest in setting as well in their pursuit of a good, compelling story set in the past. No matter how much readers want to lose themselves in a story, if they seek their pleasure in the realm of historical fiction, they obviously have some interest in reading about historical times and events. "Story" and "setting" cannot be thought of as entirely separate appeal factors when it comes to historical fiction.

That said, the historical novels cited and annotated in this chapter "specialize" in telling a good story.

Cannot Bridge the Gap

These novels deal with stories of cultural, racial, and religious divisions in society that, despite good intentions on the part of some individuals, simply cannot be overcome.

Baldiel, David.
  The Secret Purposes. **2005.** Morrow. 416pp. ISBN 0-06-076582-8.

German persecution of Jews in the months and years prior to the outbreak of World War II is the wellspring of this sobering novel, but its specific focus is unique—the British internment of German residents in the United Kingdom after war was declared, on the relatively secure Isle of Man. The too-quickly-forgotten plight of these internees is given a contemporary airing through the actions affecting, and the reactions of, the main character, Isaac Fabian. Isaac is the son of a rabbi in Germany, who married a Christian woman and fled the approaching anti-Semitic storm to Cambridge. Prejudice assumes a very human face here; Isaac's uneasiness in Germany and as a more-or-less prisoner in England is given distinct dimension and texture in the reader's mind.

Fisher, Vardis.
  Children of God. **1939.** Opal Laurel Holmes Publisher. 496pp. ISBN 0-918522-50-1.

This prolific American fiction writer penned at least one lasting novel, which has achieved classic status, in *Children of God*, which follows the migration of the Mormons from New York to Nauvoo, Illinois, and then finally to their permanent home in Utah. Fisher's fictionalized embellishment of the epic journey renders the story of Joseph Smith and Brigham Young and their followers not *less* realistic but decidedly *more*. In the 1820s, Smith had a vision that made him believe he was a prophet of the Lord, but after founding the Church of Latter-Day Saints, he was no longer safe in New York. As his followers moved westward, they were subjected to abuse and persecution for their beliefs. Years later, after enduring much trouble because of their practice of polygamy, the Mormons had learned the hard lesson of living as *part of* and not *apart from* the surrounding community.

French, Albert L.
  Billy. **1993.** Penguin. paper. 224pp. ISBN 0-14-017908-9.

This first novel describes, in stark regional dialect, an unsettling situation: In 1937, Billy, a black 10-year-old, is convicted and executed for the murder of a white girl in Mississippi. French shows an intense understanding of Billy's character, marking the effects of racism when it is not a subtle attitude but a catalyst of brutality. A rapidly paced and even searing novel about institutionalized injustice made even more poignant by the example of a confused child-victim.

Gurnah, Abdulrazak.
Desertion. **2005.** Pantheon. 272pp. ISBN 0-375-42354-0.

This generational saga tells an indelible tale of desertion; not, in this case, of soldiers from their ranks, but more universally, of individuals with whom one had established connections of love. The story begins in Zanzibar, in East Africa, in 1899. European colonialism is at its height. Englishman Martin Pearce is found nearly dead at the edge of the desert, and subsequently enters into a liaison with the sister of the man who rescued him. The story is essentially about cross-cultural relationships, all portrayed in sour tones because of the difficulties, for whites and blacks and Christians and Muslims in that era, of defending and sustaining integration. A second "case" follows in the 1950s, when Martin's granddaughter becomes involved in a similarly illicit-seeming relationship.

Phillips, Caryl.
Dancing in the Dark. **2005.** Knopf. 224pp. ISBN 1-4000-4396-4.

With his trademark eloquence and elegance, as well as penetrating vision of character and understanding of history, Phillips, in his eighth novel, brings back to life a legendary black performer in the early twentieth century, Burt Williams. Williams wore blackface and did the cakewalk, and Phillips graphically and poignantly illumines the damage done to the soul by such racial accommodation—ensuring that white people are not made uncomfortable by a black presence. Beneath the stage lights of Harlem, to which whites flocked, the rigid system of racism still held sway.

Yarbrough, Steve.
Visible Spirits. **2001.** Vintage. paper. 288pp. ISBN 0-375-72577-6.

In Loring, Mississippi, a small Delta town, it is the year 1902. Slavery may be long over, but inherent tensions between the races still resonate and can still dictate how lives are led in Loring. When the dissipated—and reactionary—son of a local planter, who is also the brother of the more liberal mayor and editor of the newspaper, returns to town and stirs up racial problems, hopefully to his advantage (taking away the black postmistress's job, which he wants for himself), the consequences reach all the way to President Teddy Roosevelt's office. A poignant, well-informed depiction of the difficult and delayed transition between the Old and New South.

From the Other Side: Alternate Viewpoints

Call it alternate history or speculative history, the historical novel offers a golden opportunity to pose the question, what if? The creative answers provided by the following authors make intriguing storylines through which to visit history as it *might* have happened.

Dann, Jack.
> *The Rebel: An Imagined Life of James Dean.* **2004.** Morrow. 416pp. ISBN 0-380-97839-3.
>
>> In this intriguing piece of speculative history, the author imagines actor James Dean surviving his car crash in 1955. As Dann has it, Dean goes on to make a political career for himself. A clever and compelling novel; it may at first seem too unreal a story, but it becomes a very real one.

Gingrich, Newt, and William R. Forstchen.
> *Gettysburg.* **2003.** St. Martin's/Thomas Dunne. 384pp. ISBN 0-312-30935-X; St. Martin's Griffin. paper. 480pp. ISBN 0-312-30936-8.
> *Grant Comes East.* **2004.** St. Martin's/Thomas Dunne. 400pp. ISBN 0-312-30937-6.
> *Never Call Retreat.* **2005.** St. Martin's/Thomas Dunne. 496pp. ISBN 0-312-34298-5.
>
>> The former Speaker of the U.S. House of Representatives and now a historian, and his historian coauthor, present a staggering, believable trilogy of alternate versions of the Civil War. In the first title, they have General Robert E. Lee winning at Gettysburg, and in the second they follow plausible consequences—the threat on Washington, D.C., in particular—if such a Confederate victory had actually occurred. The concluding volume posits a different end to the war: The general outcome is the same, but *how* the outcome came to be is given an alternative twist.

Roth, Philip.
> *The Plot Against America.* **2004.** Houghton. 400pp. ISBN 0-618-50928-3.
>
>> One of the most preeminent contemporary American writers has penned a provocative, disturbing, intelligent, and impossible-to-put-down "what-if" novel, in which he imagines the consequences on, primarily, the American Jewish community if aviation hero Charles Lindbergh had been elected president of the United States in 1940. Lindbergh, in real life, was pro-fascist and an admirer of Hitler. A stunning achievement, greatly applauded by critics upon its publication.

Stevenson, Jane.
The Empress of the Last Days. **2004.** Houghton. 369pp. ISBN 0-618-14974-7.

Although it takes place in the present day, this concluding volume in the author's trilogy, begun with *The Winter Queen* and continued in *The Shadow King,* is so rooted in history, springing forth from the situations explored in its predecessors, that it qualifies to be listed as historical fiction. The premise here is that a black scientist living in Barbados is the rightful queen of Great Britain, based on her descent from Elizabeth of Bohemia, sister of England's Charles I, and her second (clandestinely married) husband, a black African prince and former slave. The results of such a discovery make for a creatively imagined story.

Turtledove, Harry.
Return Engagements. **2004.** Del Rey. 640pp. ISBN 0-345-45723-4.

The author has enjoyed a popular career writing novels offering varia-tions on American history, and this title inaugurates a trilogy called Settling Accounts. It opens in the early stages of World War II. America as we know it does not exist; the Confederacy won the Civil War, and it has survived, even up to the opening salvos of World War II. Nor is Canada the Canada we know, and the Holocaust is a whole different matter here. A truly provocative book.

Updike, John.
Gertrude and Claudius. **2000.** Ballantine. paper. 212pp. ISBN 0-449-00697-2.

Updike's version of Shakespeare's *Hamlet* is an intelligent—albeit per-haps overwritten—imagining of what transpired before the action of the bard's play begins: in other words, a prequel to the famous drama, showing how events lead up to what happens in the play. The reader is treated to Updike's provocative psychological profiles of Queen Gertrude and King Claudius, with Prince Hamlet actually taking a back seat here, not, as in the famous play, the center of messy Danish court politics, which the author captures with an authoritative ring.

Against the Odds: Acts of Courage

Triumph over adversity is always inspiring to read about, from personal tri-umph over the limits of one's background and societal prejudice to an individ-ual's triumph over oppression.

Bass, Rick.
The Diezmo. **2005.** Houghton. 208pp. ISBN 0-395-92617-3.

Set in nineteenth-century Texas during the short "window" of history when it was an independent republic. In old age, Bass's narrator, James

Alexander, recalls his exciting time as a militia member, summoned to service by the legendary president of Texas, Sam Houston, and sent off to the Rio Grande to guard against further encroachment by Mexican forces. The militia were captured and held in deplorable conditions, but obviously Alexander survived to tell his tale.

Bell, Madison Smartt.

All Soul's Rising. **1995.** Penguin. paper. 530pp. ISBN 0-14-25947-3.

This powerful novel began a trilogy (followed by *The Master of the Crossroads* and *The Stone That the Builder Refused*) about the life and influence of second-generation African slave Toussaint-Louverture, leader of a successful slave revolt in the 1790s that ended French rule in Haiti. Intelligent, gorgeously written, historically precise, psychologically discerning, and dramatic to the ultimate degree—this is a complete package for the reader.

Faber, Michael.

The Crimson Petal and the White. **2002.** Harcourt. 848pp. ISBN 0-15-100692-X; Harvest. paper. 920pp. ISBN 0-15-602877-8.

Heavily detailed, giving the reader a wide-angled, dramatic picture of Victorian London in the 1870s, Faber's novel follows the course taken by Sugar, a clever, intelligent prostitute, as she sets out to escape her dismal, dangerous life. Populated by colorful, well-drawn characters, this is an absolutely riveting reading experience, and the reader is completely drawn into Sugar's plight.

Haulsey, Kuwana.

Angel of Harlem. **2004.** Ballantine/One World. 352pp. ISBN 0-345-50870-8.

In the 1920s, Dr. May Chinn was in the vanguard of women entering the medical profession, and she became a noted specialist in cancer treatment. This novelization of her life places her experiences within the exciting and, here, vividly drawn context of the Harlem Renaissance, the black arts movement centered in Harlem in the 1920s and 1930s. This first-person account reconstructs a lifelong struggle against racist and gender restraints on personal success, amounting to a riveting and ultimately heartbreaking story of never letting go of one's dreams.

Hawthorne, Nathaniel.

The Scarlet Letter. **1850.** Bantam. paper. 256pp. ISBN 0-553-21009-2.

The Great American Novel? Many critics believe so. Regardless, it has remained a timeless tale of the consequences of sin, set in colonial Massachusetts. Hester Prynne is found guilty of adultery and is condemned to wear a scarlet "A" on her breast. But as events unfold, the symbol of her public humiliation eventually becomes a badge of honor. Many people had to read this in high school and found it not to their liking. Have adult fiction readers try it again; it is definitely for grown-up appreciators of literary fiction.

Llywelyn, Morgan.
<u>**Irish Century series.**</u>

> *1916: A Novel of the Irish Rebellion.* **1998.** Forge. paper. 576pp. ISBN 0-8125-7492-3.
>
> *1921: The Great Novel of the Irish Civil War.* **2001.** Forge. paper. 560pp. ISBN 0-8125-7079-0.
>
> *1949.* **2003.** Forge. paper. 512pp. ISBN 0-8125-7080-4.
>
> *1972: A Novel of Ireland's Unfinished Revolution.* **2005.** Forge. paper. 384pp. ISBN 0-312-87857-5.
>
> > The first four entries in the author's <u>Irish Century series</u> track the course of Ireland's fight for independence throughout the twentieth century. Each novel focuses on a crucial juncture in that struggle: in 1916, the Easter Rising, when a handful of individuals held out for a while against the far superior strength of the British army; in 1921, the Irish Civil War, waged between supporters and opponents of the partition of Ireland into the free South and the British-ruled North; in 1949, the proclamation of the Republic of Ireland, completely disassociated from any connections with Britain; and in 1972, the "Troubles" between the Catholic minority and Protestant majority in Northern Ireland. Events are refracted through the lives and experiences of people involved in the brave fight, both real and fictitious; the calling card of these novels is putting a personal face on history, which explains their popularity and ensures a continued readership. In other words, Lywelyn makes the struggle for independence a personal, individual matter, not simply a state one. The feel of a repressed land seething with disgruntlement is palpable on every page.

Shaara, Jeff.

> *The Glorious Cause.* **2002.** Ballantine/Fawcett. paper. 704pp. ISBN 0-345-42758-0.
>
> > A sequel to the author's *Rise to Rebellion*, which was set just before the outbreak of the American Revolution, this novel follows the story from the declaration to the securing of independence. That seven-year struggle is here told primarily through the experiences of four important real-life individuals: George Washington, Benjamin Franklin, Lord Charles Cornwallis (a leading British general), and Nathanael Greene (an important American general).

Styron, William.

> *The Confessions of Nat Turner.* **1967.** Vintage. paper. 480pp. ISBN 0-679-73663-8.
>
> > Nat Turner's Revolt, as it was called, was ultimately unsuccessful, but it stirred up and spread great terror across the countryside in the South. Styron

sees the event's resonant implications for race relations. This major twentieth-century American writer delivered a magnificent, monumental, and truly
epic (but also controversial, since the author, a white man, gave expression to
a black man's consciousness) wallop with the publication of this novel based
on an actual insurrection of black slaves in a remote region of Virginia in
1831.

Coming of Age

A timeless theme is played out in various circumstances in historical fiction—
individualized sets of events make each coming-of-age story unique.

Cofer, Judith.
The Meaning of Consuelo. **2003.** Farrar. 200pp. ISBN 0-374-20509-4.

> The time is the 1950s, and in Puerto Rico young Consuelo must decide
> the nature of her own future: support her increasingly dysfunctional family or
> become an outsider in traditional Puerto Rican culture—which, in the face of
> the increasing presence of *American* culture, is on the wane. The teenage
> years are difficult enough without one's family going through domestic tur-
> moil *and* the land of one's youth undergoing significant transformation, from
> old ways to brand new ones.

Just, Ward.
An Unfinished Season. **2004.** Houghton. 251pp. ISBN 0-618-03669-5.

> Set in suburban Chicago in the 1950s, the prolific Just's fourteenth
> novel is a coming-of-age story about a 19-year-old boy whose parents' mar-
> riage is collapsing. He spends the summer days before entering the Univer-
> sity of Chicago at a tabloid newspaper with regular working-class reporters
> and his nights at North Shore country-club dances, where he meets the
> daughter of a provocative, puzzling psychiatrist. An event occurs that soon
> propels the boy headlong into a more mature understanding of real life and
> the realities of social hierarchy.

Leffland, Ella.
Rumors of Peace. **1979.** Perennial. paper. 400pp. ISBN 0-06-091301-0.

> During the four long years in which the United States was involved in
> World War II, a young girl in a small town in California comes to young
> womanhood. The horrible events of the outside world have a great impact on
> her growing awareness of human nature, from her mother's response to the
> German invasion of Denmark, where she has relatives, to trying to outgrow
> an adolescent crush on a German-Jewish college student. In the middle of all
> this, she discusses universal teenage girl things with her girlfriends.

Loh, Vyvyane.

   Breaking the Tongue. **2004.** Norton. 448pp. ISBN 0-393-05792-5; Norton. paper. 416pp. ISBN 0-393-32654-3.

      World War II–era Singapore provides a rich setting for the intricate story of Claude Lim, Chinese by descent but in whose family only English is spoken—an act "bespeaking" their desire to please and imitate the colonizers. As the Japanese lay siege to Singapore, Claude must mix with the locals and face his true heritage, but his being fluent only in English is a barrier to bridging the gap.

Morris, Willie.

   Taps. **2001.** Houghton. 352pp. ISBN 0-618-09859-3; Mariner. paper. 352pp. ISBN 0-618-21902-1.

      A beautifully effective, poignant but not maudlin, coming-of-age story set in the author's native Mississippi during the Korean War, by the late Morris, who died in 1999 and who was a favorite raconteur of the American popular reading public. This novel is basically about a 16-year-old boy who plays taps at the funerals of local soldiers who have died on the battlefield, but also about the teenager experiencing love, sex, and jealousy, all rendered in rich detail.

Sa, Shan.

   The Girl Who Played Go. **2003.** Vintage. paper. 288pp. ISBN 1-4000-3228-8.

      Coming of age is a difficult proposition even in the most comfortable of circumstances; in wartime, when one's very country is in peril, the process involves further complications. A teenage Chinese girl living in Japanese-occupied Manchuria in the 1930s attracts, at the advent of womanhood, the attention of a Japanese soldier in disguise. In brief chapters alternating their points of view, their combined story achieves, in the author's beautifully controlled writing style, an aching delicacy despite the increasingly bleak and even dangerous events transpiring around them. Growing up is essentially a universal experience, but the version told here is not a cliché.

Domestic Drama

    Families always have bickered, and will continue to do so, even to the point of open warfare; these stories are naturally filled with drama and action.

Jakes, John.

   North and South. **1982.** Signet. paper. 812pp. ISBN 0-451-20081-0.

      This is the first volume of a trilogy by a best-selling author, which was followed by *Love and War* (1984) and *Heaven and Hell* (1987). These volumes define "panorama" and "epic," bringing a bounty of authentic detail and fast pacing to the story of two families divided by the war that, for four years, threatened to tear the nation asunder. This novel is just the ticket for readers who prefer rapid movement through a fictional narrative over subtlety of plot and careful, deliberate character development.

Maine, David.
   Fallen. 2005. St. Martin's. 256pp. ISBN 0-312-32849-4.
   Biblical stories provide source material for the author of *The Preservationist* (see below). This time he brings his narrative talents and proven ability to vivify rather figurative biblical characters, pumping them full of pulsing blood, to his interpretation of Cain and Abel's contention-filled relationship. Events are told in reverse order; "real" time in this yarn is Cain's old age. He recalls the murder and the divine punishment it incurred, then Abel has his turn at narration, sharing his perspective from the point in time of just prior to his murder. Adam and Eve then chime in with their contribution to the story, as aging parents. Not only does Maine imbue his biblically based novels with genuine and appropriate humor, he succeeds in making these stories real domestic dramas. The settings are far removed from today, but the family dynamics are decidedly not. Therein lies his novels' double appeal.

Maine, David.
   The Preservationist. 2004. St. Martin's. paper. 240pp. ISBN 0-312-32847-8.
   The timeless and ever-dramatic biblical story of Noah and his ark is retold, with humor and impressive realism, as a family drama. This is a tale of Noe (as it is spelled here) and his faith in God, with first-person accounts by Noe's wife and sons and daughters-in-laws. Characters come to full, viable life in this graphic account of many months afloat, with no apparent relief in sight.

Mann, Thomas.
   Joseph and His Brothers. 1933–1943. Everyman's Library. 1,492pp. ISBN 1-4000-4001-9.
   By the great, Nobel Prize–winning German writer, this tetralogy is known collectively as *Joseph and His Brothers,* but each volume was originally published separately: *The Stories of Jacob* (1933), *Young Joseph* (1934), *Joseph in Egypt* (1936), and *Joseph the Provider* (1943). As the titles indicate, these four novels tell the biblical story of Joseph—and expand on what information there is in the Bible itself. The great detail—readers fairly breathe in the air of ancient Egypt and the Holy Land—is matched by the author's intense probing and immaculate understanding of the main character's psychology as well as, on a loftier plane, the role of myth in tribal functions. But this is not a soulless, intellectual depiction, and the family drama here is universal despite the specific context in which it unfolds.

Rutherfurd, Edward.

Sarum. **1987.** Fawcett. paper. 912pp. ISBN 0-449-00072-9.

Rutherford's big, sprawling novels are prime examples of the "epic." This, his first one, offers nothing less than a complete history of England from the Ice Age to modern times, as reflected by and refracted through the lives of several generations of a handful of families, with all their ups and downs, tensions and familiarities, and private battles and public unities. The focal point of this extremely detailed narrative (but which nevertheless rings with real life) is the old city of Sarum, now known as Salisbury.

West, Rebecca.

The Fountain Overflows. **1956.** New York Review of Books. paper. 408pp. ISBN 1-59017-034-2.

West, an esteemed British journalist, critic, and fiction and travel writer, outdid herself in this indisputably absorbing depiction of the domestic concerns, issues, delights, and escapes of a middle-class Edwardian family in financial decline. A beautifully layered picture of the customs and attitudes of the time and milieu, at a time when keeping up appearances was a life struggle.

Almost Forever

Readers should plan to spend a long time reading and luxuriating in these novels, which, although they seem to go on and on, ultimately are worth the time spent within their pages.

Dumas, Alexandre.

The Count of Monte-Cristo. **1844.** Pocket. paper. 688pp. ISBN 0-7434-8755-9.

This classic of French literature is pure story over every other appeal factor, and what a great adventure story it is. Despite relatively flat character-izations, this novel still rivets readers' attention as they follow the exploits of Edmond Dantès, who is imprisoned for several years on trumped-up charges but gets his revenge when he escapes, locating a vast fortune about which he'd been told while jailed, and thus transfigures himself into the wealthy Count of Monte-Cristo.

Mitchell, Margaret.

Gone with the Wind. **1936.** Avon. paper. 1,024pp. ISBN 0-380-00109-8.

Could this be the Great American *historical* novel? More people have seen the movie, perhaps, than read the book, but a summer vacation by the beach is the perfect venue for finally getting around to enjoying *on paper* the plights and survival strategies of spoiled and petty Scarlet O'Hara, who, in the face of extreme forces tearing her world apart, must discover the gumption within herself to avoid sinking in the South of the Civil War and Reconstruction.

Scott, Walter.

Ivanhoe. **1820.** Tor. paper. 544pp. ISBN 0-8125-6565-7.

One of the classics of English literature as well as enduringly popular, Scott's chivalric adventure story is set in twelfth-century England and draws on the personalities and exploits of two very dramatic and legendary heroes, Richard the Lionheart, the king who has just returned from the Crusades, and Robin Hood—and we all know what his deal was. Plus, there is the romance between the knight Ivanhoe and the fair Lady Rowena. Captivating in its plot twists and turns, with tournament flags flying and damsels in need of . . . well, you know.

Thackeray, William.

Henry Esmond. **1852.** Oxford University. paper. 493pp. ISBN 0-19-282727-8.

Thackeray is a major figure in Victorian literature. For this carefully painted canvas he looked back to late-seventeenth and early-eighteenth-century England. The eponymous character is the ward of a viscount, who loses his life in battle trying to restore the House of Stuart to the British throne. Later, in the army, Henry earns distinction; ultimately, his love for two women comes to very satisfactory fruition, and the reader has been occupied by a rewarding reading experience.

Tolstoy, Leo.

War and Peace. **1865–1869.** Penguin. paper. 1,472pp. ISBN 0-14-044417-3.

The "mother" of all novels, the novel everyone plans to read someday, this epic is daunting in its size, scope, and large cast of characters. A fact that is often forgotten, however, is that it is a *historical* novel, written six decades after the time in which it is set: the Napoleonic era, especially what the French emperor and his lust for conquest and territory wrought in the Russian Empire. A greatly involved plot reflects the complications of Russian society, foreign relations, and the French invasion of Mother Russia—and just plain human nature, which is what ultimately makes this huge novel so compelling.

Wallace, Lew.

Ben Hur. **1880.** Signet. paper. 558pp. ISBN 0-14-515287-3.

You've seen the movie, of course, so now read the book. Chances are, most readers will get even more involved in the print version of this richly written, highly dramatic tale of the scion of a distinguished Jewish family in Jerusalem at the time of Christ and how, after many trials and tribulations, he is converted to Christianity.

Wouk, Herman.

The Winds of War. **1971.** Back Bay. paper. 885pp. ISBN 0-316-95266-4.

War and Remembrance. **1978.** Back Bay. paper. 1,042pp. ISBN 0-316-95499-3.

These classic war novels, published seven years apart, are nevertheless a two-part story. The general focus is World War II and the years immediately before and after it; the specific focal point is how these global and life-altering events affected the members of one family. Wouk's settings reach the world over, and his historical concerns are wide: from incredible events in the Holocaust to presidential deliberations in the White House to what transpires on a battleship and in a submarine or bomber. Characters are not incidental to his reconstruction of events; they pulse with realism and propel the reader through the many pages of these partner novels.

Politics as Usual

Few things in life are certain, but in addition to death and taxes, there is the certainty that humans are political creatures, and that politics will always be conducted, well, politically.

Donoghue, Emma.

Little Mask. **2004.** Harcourt. 672pp. ISBN 0-15-100943-0.

Based on the lives of three historical figures, this intriguing novel conveys, with minute but colorful and certainly never tedious detail, the atmosphere of eighteenth-century London. The author zeroes in on a love triangle (one man, a wealthy lord; his actress mistress; and her purportedly "Sapphist" friend, a sculptress) that erupts into scandal. Sex and politics—perennially intersecting issues in any capital city—are portrayed here with authority and élan.

George, Margaret.

Mary Queen of Scots and the Isles. **1992.** St. Martin's/Griffin. paper. 880pp. ISBN 0-312-15585-9.

Another in the author's series of lengthy fictional biographies of significant historical figures, this one brings onto the stage one of the most dramatic royal lives in European history, that of the ill-fated Stuart queen of Scotland. George finds Queen Mary's political problems rooted in her personality flaws, including her impetuosity; the result is an authentic depiction of turbulent sixteenth-century Scottish and English politics, during which time religious issues and the likelihood of a Catholic succession to Protestant Elizabeth I's throne dominated life in both countries.

Kennedy, William.
Roscoe. **2002.** Penguin. paper. 306pp. ISBN 0-14-200173-2.

This is the seventh and latest in Kennedy's highly regarded series of novels set in the historical past in Albany, New York; along with *Ironweed*, it is considered the most powerful novel in the cycle. Here, World War II has just ended, and Roscoe Conway, long-time second-in-command of Albany's Democratic machine, is making efforts to extricate himself from the system. In his typical flinty yet elegant prose style and with an understanding of characters who are good people at heart, Kennedy brilliantly illuminates the dark side of politics.

Tremain, Rose.
Music & Silence. **2000.** Washington Square. paper. 485pp. ISBN 0-7434-1826-3.

Winner of the prestigious British Whitbread Prize, this marvelously complex novel by a highly regarded writer of literary historical novels takes readers to a setting rarely explored by American and British fiction writers: seventeenth-century Denmark. An English lutist travels to the court of King Christian IV to be a member of the royal orchestra; there he becomes embroiled in both court intrigue and a difficult romance with a lady attendant to the king's wife. The story is told from multiple points of view, which adds to the richness of the style and the depth of the characterizations; the result is a many-layered story with multiple appeals.

Vidal, Gore.
Washington, D.C. **1967.** Vintage. paper. 432pp. ISBN 0-375-70877-4.

This volume in Vidal's highly knowledgeable, boldly intelligent, and extremely stylish <u>Chronicles of America</u> series of historical novels, in which he masterfully mixes real and fictional characters focuses on the nation's capital and the American political system (with emphasis on how power corrupts) as illustrated by the career of one James Borden Day, a conservative Southern senator who is a presidential hopeful.

Warren, Robert Penn.
All the King's Men. **1946.** Harvest. paper. 456pp. ISBN 0-15-600480-1.

How grassroots politics works and the morality of the populist politician are the exciting issues probed in this novel based (but not so obviously that it comes off as a gimmick or a pseudo-biography) on the life of Louisiana's most (in)famous twentieth-century political figure, Governor Huey P. Long. He is called Willie Stark here, and the point of this successfully filmed novel (starring Broderick Crawford in the major role) is that power corrupts; in the process of Warren's development of this theme, the reader is treated to high drama.

Action-Packed Adventures

There are twists and turns aplenty in these roller-coaster yarns that keep you going full tilt to the last page.

Boyd, James.
Drums. **1925.** Atheneum. 430pp. ISBN 0-689-80176-9.

> The American Revolution has proven to be a rich vein for historical novelists to mine, and this novel, set during that critical time, is a classic in the genre of historical fiction. Boyd's emphasis is adventure, focusing on the son of a North Carolina planter, who obtains a good education in preparation for being a gentleman then travels to London, where he spends time working in an import firm. But while there he decides to enlist in the fledgling American navy, struggling against the mother country.

Chadwick, Elizabeth.
The Falcons of Montabard. **2004.** St. Martin's. 480pp. ISBN 0-312-33208-4.

> This is quite an adventure yarn, mixing historical and fictional characters in a compelling stew set in the twelfth century, from Scotland to the Near East. Crusading knights, romantic dalliances, border raids, and kidnappings and subsequent demands for ransom all play a role, ensuring readers a colorful and fast-paced narrative to spend some easy hours enjoying.

Clavell, James.
Shogun. **1975.** Dell. paper. 1,152pp. ISBN 0-440-17800-2.

> This sprawling but compelling saga continues to enthrall readers three decades after its publication. With an eye to drama, Clavell whisks readers off to an inherently dramatic place and time: seventeenth-century Japan, riven by feuding overlords. Into this hostile mix come an English sea pilot and his crew, their ship tossed ashore in Japan.

Cornwell, Bernard.
Sharpe's Eagle. **1981.** Signet. paper. 288pp. ISBN 0-451-21257-6.

> Cornwell began his ever-popular series featuring Richard Sharpe, a Napoleonic-era soldier-adventurer, with this novel, which introduced traits that would characterize all the Sharpe novels to come: dramatic and authentic battle scenes and a highly charged and energetic prose style that correlates perfectly with the exciting plot. The first volume and its successors are historical adventure of the first degree.

Dumas, Alexandre.
The Three Musketeers. **1844.** Bantam. paper. 560pp. ISBN 0-55-321337-7.

Adventure tales set in the past do not come any more spirited and compelling and just plain "drama over the top" than this classic novel about royal romance and intrigue set in the seventeenth-century court of Louis XIII and featuring the three guardsmen, Athos, Porthos, and Aramis. Incorporated into their "buddy-circle" is a fourth musketeer, D'Artagnan. Talk about a classic novel that has withstood the test of time: Swords and ladies, kings and knaves; how can the reader go wrong?

Fraser, George MacDonald.
Flashman. **1969.** Plume. paper. 256pp. ISBN 0-452-25961-4.

Fraser began his series of adventuresome, highly entertaining novels starring Sir Henry Flashman, soldier of fortune and adventurer in the Victorian era, with this irresistible novel. The premise of the series is that Fraser is editing the personal papers/memoirs of Flashman for publication. The result is a cycle of fast, absorbing, and colorful yarns that will keep the reader up till the wee hours.

McKenna, Richard.
The Sand Pebbles. **1962.** Naval Institute Press. paper. 624pp. ISBN 1-55750-446-6.

More people these days have seen the marvelously effective 1966 movie version of this novel, starring Steve McQueen and Candice Bergen, than have actually read it (although it garnered critical acclaim upon its publication and appeared on the *New York Times* best-seller list). *Read it!* In 1920s China, after the fall of the imperial regime and now in a state of civil war, as warlord goes up against warlord, the U.S. gunboat *San Pablo* patrols the upper Yangtze River, as a show of American intentions to protect American missionaries and business interests. Its very presence is antagonist to the Chinese factions, who want no outside interference in their domestic affairs. A new crew member's growing awareness of Chinese culture, and his burgeoning sensitivities and sensibilities, have a major impact on the *San Pablo*'s crew. The creak of the old gunboat as it plows the river is mixed with the shouts of fury from the riverbanks—the noise of an old, old nation finding its new way.

Reade, Charles.
The Cloister and the Hearth. **1861.** Wildside Press. paper. 292pp. ISBN 1-59224-922-1.

Reade was a scholar and barrister in Victorian times, as well as a novelist, producing, while wearing the latter hat, one lasting novel, the classic *Cloister and Hearth*. Fifteenth-century continental European life springs to life in his fluid prose, resting authentically on careful research. Readers can virtually hear the arrows zooming past their ears as they embark on this luxuriously detailed excursion into how life could easily become a cycle of twists and turns in the tumultuous European politics of the day. Events focus on Gerard Eliason, a young Dutch artist, whose patron is Margaret Van Eyck, sister of the famous painter Jan Van Eyck. Romantic entanglements and a set of adventures in the company of a soldier from the duchy of Burgundy are Gerard's to "enjoy." His son grows up to be the famous biblical scholar Erasmus.

Roberts, Kenneth.

Arundel. **1930.** Down East Books. paper. 486pp. ISBN 0-89272-364-5.

Rubble in Arms. **1933.** Down East Books. paper. 586pp. ISBN 0-89272-386-6.

Northwest Passage. **1937.** Down East Books. paper. 712pp. ISBN 0-89272-542-7.

An author who is unfortunately little read these days—in fact, he is unfamiliar to most contemporary readers—Roberts nevertheless enjoyed an excellent reputation in the 1930s to 1950s, and he was awarded a special career-spanning Pulitzer Prize in 1957. His novels deal with American history from the French and Indian War to the War of 1812, from Colonel Benedict Arnold's secret march on Quebec in 1775 (in *Arundel*) to the battles of 1776 and 1777 (in *Rabble in Arms*) to the exploits of Major Robert Rogers in the French and Indian War and his desire to discover a passage to the Pacific (in *Northwest Passage*). Roberts's tales are epic in scope and flow with great speed, charting the tidal wave of history at an important time in colonial North America and the new American republic, but they are remarkable, too, for personalizing history—for creating viable personalities out of both historical and fictional figures.

Before You Know It: Quick Reads

These novels are not necessarily quick because they are slight or especially short, but because of the author's ability to create a riveting storyline without using difficult language or complicated plotting. In other words, the end comes too soon.

Cornwell, Bernard.

The Last Kingdom. **2005.** HarperCollins. 352pp. ISBN 0-06-053051-0.

With this exciting novel, the author of the ever-popular <u>Richard Sharpe</u> series (see *Sharpe's Eagle*) inaugurates a brand new series of historical novels, this one set in medieval England. This is Anglo-Saxon England, before it was united into the kingdom we know today. The small realms of

Northumbria, East Anglia, Murcia, and Wessex struggle in civil war and resist Danish invasion. Heroic warriors and blood feuds give the novel its mesmerizing action and swift pace.

Hope, Anthony.
The Prisoner of Zenda/Rupert of Hentzau. **1894, 1898.** Penguin. paper. 400pp. ISBN 0-14-043755-X.

The Prisoner of Zenda remains one of the most popular novels of all time, and understandably so, for it is a fast-paced, swashbuckling yarn about an Englishman who impersonates the king of "Ruritania" at His Majesty's coronation, to stave off a plot to remove him from the throne. The reader cannot help but be immediately swept up into the action and charm of this story. The sequel—in just as spirited and ingratiating a manner and at the same double-quick time as its predecessor—follows the Englishman's further Ruritanian adventures, centering on his falling in love with the king's fiancée.

Jakes, John.
Savannah; or, A Gift from Mr. Lincolcn. **2004.** Dutton. 304pp. ISBN 0-525-94803-1.

Jakes specializes in lightweight fictional re-creations of the Civil War era, resting on adequate factual accuracy but at the same time going only surface deep in his portrayal of events, characters, and political and social issues. Nevertheless, he is popular for a reason: namely, an easy and energetic reading experience that imparts enough of a general picture of the period for casual readers. This particular novel brings back the winter of the year 1864, in Savannah, Georgia; Union General William T. Sherman is engaged in his infamous campaign to devastate Georgia, just having burned Atlanta. The smoke of destruction fairly wafts off these pages.

Shaara, Jeff.
Gone for Soldiers. **2000.** Ballantine. paper. 512pp. ISBN 0-345-42752-1.

Shaara, son of Michael Shaara, author of the Pulitzer Prize–winning and now-classic Civil War novel *The Killer Angels*, here turns his equally assured storytelling eye on the Mexican War in 1847. American forces under General Winfield Scott land at Vera Cruz and work their way up to the Mexican capital, their adversary being the dictator General Antonio López de Santa Anna. Vivid details of battle scenes are matched by the author's perceptiveness about the soldiers' and commanders' mindsets (many of the latter figure later as leaders, on opposing sides, in the Civil War).

Silber, Joan.

Ideas of Heaven: A Ring of Stories. **2004.** Norton. paper. 250pp. ISBN 0-393-32687-X.

As noted in my introduction, "historical fiction" connotes the novel as opposed to the short story, the latter not having been a particularly successful medium for fictional re-creation of the historical past; for some reason, short stories have contemporary settings, and that's it. Well, not quite *it*. A contradiction to that maxim is this collection of stories that was a finalist for the National Book Award. As each story is read in order of appearance in the book, each of the six stories has some degree of connection to the one preceding it, and two of the six have historical settings. I include these stories here because of their short length, but they are nevertheless quite potent pieces of writing, using their historical contexts very effectively. "Gaspara Stampa," which takes place in Renaissance Italy, is about a woman poet who imbues her work with the love she feels for the man from whom she is separated; "Ideas of Haven" tracks the experiences of an American missionary family in late-nineteenth-century China, when foreigners were increasingly prevalent and increasingly at risk of being attacked by antiforeign mobs.

Stevenson, Robert Louis.

Kidnapped. **1886.** Bantam. paper. 240pp. ISBN 0-55321260-5.

Stevenson, who is a favorite writer of young readers as well as older ones, sets his classic adventure yarn—the quintessential adventure novel—in Scotland in the mid-eighteenth century. A young man who recently lost his father travels to the estate of his uncle, where he expects not only to be welcomed but also to find entrée into the gentry. But his uncle has him kidnapped—and sent as a slave bound for America. The young man makes a lasting friendship, and he and his new friend escape the ship and make their way back to Scotland. All's well that ends well, and at the end of his string of exciting adventures, the young man finds himself established in his rightful place in society.

Best War Stories of All Time

Unlike reading about travel, reading about war is better than actually being there, and the armchair soldier will lose himself or herself in these particularly engrossing war stories.

Crane, Stephen.

The Red Badge of Courage. **1895.** Tor. paper. 176pp. ISBN 0-81250-479-8.

The reader does not witness a famous battle in the American Civil War from above, as in an airplane watching the big picture of offensive and defensive plans being executed; rather, this classic novel by a beloved American writer, in reverberating prose, sees "battle," as opposed to one certain battle, through the mind of an average—scared, that is—soldier, who perceives battle as the trauma to the individual that warfare is, not simply as the win or loss it is calculated to be by commanders and politicians.

Keneally, Thomas.

Confederates. **1979.** University of Georgia. paper. 427pp. ISBN 0-8203-2263-6.

This epic novel about the American Civil War, by a critically and popularly well-received Australian novelist, sheds light on events in battle-scarred Virginia in the summer of 1862. Its focus is four individuals involved in the conflict in various fashions: a Southern nurse who is spying for the North, a British war correspondent, and two soldiers under Stonewall Jackson's command. Through them the atmosphere of war is provocatively brought home to the reader. The particularly individual perspective on just how hellish war can be is the attraction of this fictional account.

Remarque, Erich Maria.

All Quite on the Western Front. **1929.** Fawcett. paper. 295pp. ISBN 0-449-21394-3.

To be more accurate, this is one of the best *anti*-war novels of all time. Technically not historical fiction, since it was written only a decade after the time in which it was set, this classic novel, by a German author who was a soldier in World War I, is a highly effective depiction of the horrors of life for the ordinary soldier in the trenches of that dreadful conflict. You wouldn't have wanted to be there.

Shaara, Jeff.

To the Last Man. **2004.** Ballantine. 672pp. ISBN 0-345-46134-7; paper. 672pp. ISBN 0-345-46136-3.

Son of Michael Shaara, the well-known and prize-winning author of *The Killer Angels* (see below), Jeff Shaara here turns in an admirably skilled depiction of military campaigns on the Western Front in the seemingly interminable years of World War I. Trench warfare was absolutely horrible, and through the personal perspective of the characters—Shaara emphasizes four historical figures from both sides of the conflict—the horrors are made palpable.

Sienkiewicz, Henryk.

With Fire and Sword. **1884.** Fredonia. paper. 452pp. ISBN 1-4101-0057-X.
The Deluge. **1886.** Fredonia. paper. 673pp. ISBN 1-58963-019-X.
Pan Michael. **1887.** Fredonia. paper. 548pp. ISBN 1-58963-287-7.

This Polish writer (see also *Quo Vadis*) won the Nobel Prize for Literature in 1905, and this trilogy, set in his native land in the seventeenth century, is a magnificent literary accomplishment and reading experience. Each novel in the sequence is lengthy, but the author achieves great fluidity and drive that never permits the reader's attention to flag. His emphasis is Poland's political and military history as the country deals with such neighbors as Sweden and Russia. A beautifully detailed pageant of Poland's wars of self-assertion.

Medical and Scientific Adventures

The ravages of disease and the discoveries that further the advance of science—this is inherently good material for the talented historical novelist.

Brooks, Geraldine.
Year of Wonders: A Novel of the Plague. **2001.** Penguin. paper. 308pp. ISBN 0-14-200143-0.

> The year is 1666—when the dreaded bubonic plague spread from London to a remote English village. The villagers quarantine themselves in a courageous effort to contain the illness. What the author has done so inventively is to imagine what life was like during this horrible time, and she depicts the universality of human response to trials and grief.

Byrd, Max.
Shooting the Sun. **2004.** Bantam. 320pp. ISBN 0-553-80208-9; Bantam. paper. 320pp. ISBN 0-553-58369-7.

> Byrd is the author of a successful suite of biographical novels about U.S. presidents (see *Grant*, *Jackson*, and *Jefferson*). In this creative, even educational novel, he borrows historical figures as well as inventing his own as he visits the 1840s to limn the effects of two scientifically minded individuals who trek to and across the American Southwest, beginning in Washington, D.C., to witness a solar eclipse.

Darton, John.
The Darwin Conspiracy. **2005.** Knopf. 320pp. ISBN 1-4000-4137-6.

> Bi- and tri-level novels featuring separate yet related storylines taking place at different time periods can set up an almost kaleidoscopic experience for the reader: a brilliant series of changing impressions mesmerizing the reader's eye. Overarching this three-tiered novel are the personality and scientific legacy of naturalist Charles Darwin and his theory of evolution. We first see Darwin as a young man growing up and voyaging on the H.M.S. *Beagle*; later, we are shown his daughter, a nascent feminist in straight-laced Victorian times; and finally, two modern scholars pursue research into the provenance of Darwin's theories. At once fast-paced and erudite.

Goldberg, Myla.
Wickett's Remedy. **2005.** Doubleday. 336pp. ISBN 0-385-51324-0.

The author of the best-selling *Bee Season* (2000) sets this novel in the early twentieth century, when Irish shopkeeper Lydia Kilkenny wants to get out of her South Boston neighborhood. Her marriage to a nice man, Henry Wickett, opens the door for her escape to a better life. Henry is training as a doctor, but he has his dreams, too: to leave school behind for a potentially lucrative business venture—much to Lydia's consternation. The Spanish influenza epidemic hits, and Lydia's life is irrevocably altered. Through various devices—such as interweaving period newspaper articles and personal correspondence—Goldberg engages the reader with an atmospheric picture of the times: Who will be coughing and sniffling tomorrow? The tension was palpable then, and is so in the pages of this novel now.

Kurzweil, Allen.
A Case of Curiosities. **1992.** Harvest. paper. 384pp. ISBN 0-15-601289-8.

At a Paris auction in the 1980s, the narrator buys a *momento hominem*, a lifebox, a box of curiosities pertaining to and illustrating the life of one person, in this case Claude Page, an eighteenth-century French clockmaker and mechanical genius. Claude endeavors to build a talking automaton. Getting to know him and his scientific endeavors is not the reader's only pleasure; as a not-incidental by-product of this rich narrative, the reader learns about the various classes and their ways of life in pre-Revolutionary France.

Smith, Diane.
Pictures from an Expedition. **2002.** Penguin. paper. 277pp. ISBN 0-14-200406-5.

Set in 1876, this novel reflects the author's abiding interest in science and the environment. The narrative is a vividly rendered recollection of a scientific illustrator, who, along with her friend, a much older man and eccentric portrait painter, ventures to Montana on a dinosaur fossil–seeking expedition. This novel displays a masterful understanding of the scientific mind, one that is fully inclusive of new surroundings, which the woman encounters on this particular adventure.

Wood, Gillen D'arcy.
Hosack's Folly: A Novel of Old New York. **2005.** Other Press. 390pp. ISBN 1-59051-162-X.

This is historical fiction with a medical bent, based on an actual yellow fever epidemic that raged in New York City in the 1820s. The main character, David Hosack, is also taken from real life—he was the physician who cared for Alexander Hamilton after his fatal duel with Aaron Burr and later the founder of Bellevue Hospital and the Columbia University Medical School. The author's first novel is an accomplished conjuring of the fearful atmosphere of crises: the disease coming from somewhere, the water gone foul (the idea of bringing fresh water into the city via an aqueduct is discussed —which really happened). Wood does an excellent job of showing the civic side of this urban crisis, where medical necessities conflict with political exigencies— containment of the infection threatens the government coverup of the situation. The sights and smells fairly waft off the page: bodies riddled with disease, the not-yet-sick stirring up dust and noise as they flee for the open road, pigs in the streets, and rats overrunning the ships in the harbor.

Take Your Time: Novels Not to Race Through

These novels don't necessarily require time and patience because of their length, but because they are bound to make the reader think.

Eco, Umberto.
The Name of the Rose. **1983.** Harcourt. 552pp. ISBN 0-15-100213-4; Harcourt. paper. 500pp. ISBN 0-15-600370-8.

    More people are familiar with this worldwide best seller through its filmed version than from having actually read it; it is a complex, difficult, yet ultimately extremely entertaining tale revolving around a murder mystery in a medieval Italian monastery. Brother William of Baskerville comes to investigate heresy but finds himself embroiled in a series of murders. Discussions of philosophy, religion, and history are the novel's ingredients, all wrapped up by a brilliant storytelling voice.

Kantor, MacKinley.
Andersonville. **1955.** Plume. paper. 768pp. ISBN 0-452-26956-3.

    This absolutely haunting novel won the Pulitzer Prize and secured the author's reputation as one of the major twentieth-century American historical novelists. Years of research into copious documentary evidence have yielded a graphic depiction of the military prison at Andersonville, Georgia, in which 50,000 Union soldiers were incarcerated and 14,000 perished. Personalization is the calling card in this fictional depiction: prisoners, commanders, and local residents alike are viably brought to life as the author investigates what people do when subjected to, and surrounded by others subjected to, confinement and deprivation.

Lagerkvist, Pär.
The Sibyl. **1956.** Vintage. paper. 160pp. ISBN 0-394-70240-9.

    The 1951 winner of the Nobel Prize in Literature, this Swedish writer is too little read, which is unfortunate, considering the power of his creative, insightful psychological investigations, keenly rendered in a fine, precise style.

This novel, one of his most famous, steps back to ancient Greece for a parable about good and evil and the human search for God. Definitely a "thought piece," it is also a compelling read.

Ruiz Zafon, Carlos.
The Shadow of the Wind. **2004.** Penguin. paper. 487pp. ISBN 0-14-303490-1.

Murder is not only mixed with mayhem but also romance to produce a mystery-shrouded, gothic-tinged, and completely riveting (and even scary) narrative set in Barcelona, Spain, at the end of World War II. (The novel was a best seller in the author's native Spain.) The plot centers on one man's obsession with a certain book and his desire to locate other works by the same author. This psychological adventure is elaborately plotted, all within the context of Franco's repressive regime.

Long Gone: The Journey or Quest

A journey does not always have to be physical; it can also be a psychological quest for acceptance—or can even be a reader's journey through a novel's delightful pages.

Holland, Cecelia.
The Firedrake. **1966.** Backinprint. paper. 180p 0-595-17582-1.

After this exceptional first novel, written when the author was quite young, Holland went on to enjoy a successful career as a historical novelist, with an avid following. This first entry in her distinguished oeuvre is set in the eleventh century. In a spare style, which achieves a brooding sense of the environment, she focuses on William of Normandy's conquest of England, with the character of William taking shape before the reader's eyes by way of the exploits of an Irish mercenary knight enlisted in William's army at the Battle of Hastings.

Ishiguro, Kazuo.
When We Were Orphans. **2000.** Vintage. paper. 352pp. ISBN 0-375-72440-0.

This gracefully presented but psychologically complex novel stands with its feet nimbly planted in two quite disparate parts of the world in the troubled 1930s, England and China. It features an English detective, Christopher Banks, who was born in the early twentieth century in Shanghai and left an orphan early in life when his parents disappeared. Two decades later, his investigative practice in London has earned him celebrity, but he is compelled to return to Shanghai to finally solve the mystery of his parents' fate. But the city is engulfed in strife between the Nationalists and Communists and the invading Japanese army—a powerful backdrop to Banks's obsessive pursuit of information about his personal life and family history.

Mendensohn, Jane.
I Was Amelia Earhart. **1996.** Random. paper. 164pp. ISBN 0-679-77636-2.

Perhaps not *the* great mystery in the history of the universe, but certainly one of the most intriguing: What ultimately became of famous pilot Amelia Earhart? It's common knowledge that she and her navigator, Fred Noonan, disappeared on their 1937 around-the-world flight, somewhere off the coast of New Guinea. Mendelsohn imagines Earhart for the most part telling her own story; the author supplies engaging background about her childhood, marriage, and aviation career up to the big flight, and that flight's unknown (but here speculated on) aftermath is what readers will be most in search of here. The pages are relatively few but the details are precise, and the development of the inherently dramatic storyline, though as fast-paced as it should be in a good adventure tale, never leaves the reader unsatisfied. An island gives Earhart and Noonan a place for landing; the rest of the story is a picture of years-long, gone-native survival. The epitome of getting away from it all.

Mosby, Katherine.
Twilight. **2005.** HarperCollins. 304pp. ISBN 0-06-621271-5.

The quest for self-realization is the theme of this stylishly rendered but also deeply heartfelt narrative about a New York debutante, with too much smarts and not enough beauty, who really doesn't want the oh-so-ordinary and oh-so-boring routines of matrimony she is expected to achieve. At the "advanced" age of 30, she breaks off her engagement and, turning her back on what her parents and "society" expect of her, she goes to Paris—these are the between-the-war years—embarking on an entirely different life. But freedom and fulfillment have their price.

Unsworth, Barry.
Pascali's Island. **1980.** Norton. paper. 192pp. ISBN 0-393-31721-8.

In 1908, on a small island in the Aegean Sea, Basil Pascali spies on his fellow countrymen. As the Ottoman Empire erodes, Basil has received regular payments for spying for the Sultan and sending his dispatches back to Constantinople. But he has had no response, *ever*. Unsworth, a Booker Prize–winning novelist, here creates a marvelous world of cosmopolitanism and mystery as Basil searches for a sense of significance in the great scheme of things.

Vanderhaeghe, Guy.
The Last Crossing. **2004.** Grove. 400pp. ISBN 0-87113-912-X; Grove. paper. 400pp. ISBN 0-8021-4175-7.

This delectable yarn displaying fast action, vibrant detail, and colorful and well-drawn characters charts the course taken by two English brothers in the late nineteenth century, who are ordered by their industrialist father to go to the American West to find their other brother, who is missing. They form a search party. The story, told from alternating points of view, encompasses not only the terrain of western America and Canada but also the personal tales of all the people involved. A Canadian best seller and prize winner, this novel cannot fail to sweep the reader along on a journey through its exciting pages.

Wallace, Randall.

Love and Honor. **2004.** Simon & Schuster. 416pp. ISBN 0-7432-6519-X.

The title gives a good indication of the swashbuckling nature of this delightful adventure novel set in late-eighteenth-century Russia. Rich in historical detail and moving at a fast pace, the story centers on a Virginia cavalryman who is dispatched by Benjamin Franklin to St. Petersburg to use his masculine wiles to convince Empress Catherine the Great *not* to aid the British in their struggle to stamp out the revolt of their American colonies.

Yourcenar, Marguerite.

The Abyss. **1968.** Farrar. paper. 600pp. ISBN 0-374-51666-9.

By the author of the classic historical novel *Memoirs of Hadrian*, this book is impeccably researched and written as well as psychologically astute about the thinking of the major character, a physician-alchemist from Bruges, Belgium. The late sixteenth century was a time of great intellectual ferment, of clashing philosophies about such nontraditional ideas as alchemy and such codes of living as religious thought. Zeno travels Europe in search of the truth amid this tumult of opinion. As beautifully styled and shaped as the novel is, it is also greatly enriching as an intellectual exercise for the reader.

Zacharius, Walter.

Songbird. **2004.** Atria. 288pp. ISBN 0-7434-8211-5.

This extremely effective depiction of the Holocaust follows the plight of a Palestinian woman who, as a teenager, is shipped, along with her family, to a concentration camp. She escapes on the way and becomes involved in the Resistance. Later she comes to the United States. Her participation in the Resistance movement is not over, however, and after the war she goes to Palestine. A gripping story of paths taken toward survival.

Chapter 4

Language

When referring to the "language" found in a novel, we are speaking about, first, the author's writing style. Is it concise and straightforward, relaxed and fluid, tight and poetic, or elaborate and verging on overwrought? Is it filled with lush metaphors and imagery, or with difficult word usage and complicated sentence structure? Is the language so easy to follow that the reader is hardly aware there even *is* a writing style? Is it so awkward that the storyline and the character presentation had better be done well, as compensation, or the reader will find it too difficult to actually proceed through the narrative?

The truth is, most readers do not pay an extraordinary amount of attention to language; or, more exactly, most readers are aware of a writer's style on a more subconscious level than that on which they perceive any other of the factors that attract their attention and pique their interest.

But concomitant to that is the fact that readers actually respond to language—style—much more keenly than they realize. A historical novel written in the way people spoke in, say, Tudor England may have more pull on a reader than its *setting* in Tudor England alone. Recognizing one's attraction to a certain fictional work based on its language "style" (not the *actual* language in which it was written, such as English or French or Czech) often takes a moment, but that thread of linkage to other novels leads to a wide and rich range of reading choices, with an extensive variety of settings, storylines, and characters. The language of a novel is one of the most intriguing ways of discovering the next novel a reader would probably enjoy, and it can most surprisingly turn up satisfying results in the pursuit, "I want another novel just like this one."

Historical fiction is especially rich in language; composing a historical novel seems to offer a novelist a tantalizing range of style choices in which to present the material.

Language, for our purposes here, can also refer to a novel's format. As evidenced in some of the categories that follow, we explore the various formats historical novelists can employ. This is the language in which an author wrote a novel as dictated by the particular format chosen for that novel.

In Journal Form

These novels assume the form of the protagonist writing a journal. Written in the first person, they offer an intimate and personal perspective on historical events.

Banville, John.
The Untouchable. **1997.** Vintage. paper. 368pp. ISBN 0-679-76747-9.

In his old age, a distinguished art historian and former spy for British intelligence is revealed to have been a spy for the Soviet Union. In his late-term exposure, he composes a journal to explain himself, in a tone at once droll, wise, and deeply understanding of the diplomacy of the times (the cold war) and of the masked personality (the main character was also gay). The novel, by a well-respected writer who is the literary editor of the *Irish Times*, firmly establishes itself on solid ground between the comedy of manners and the espionage thriller.

Elphinstone, Margaret.
Voyageurs. **2004.** Cannongate. paper. 466pp. ISBN 1-84195-643-0.

In the form of a journal written at the time when the events it covers actually occurred but now rewritten nearly three decades later, this novel, brimming with adventure, is set on the U.S.–Canadian border just before the War of 1812. The protagonist leaves his home in England (at the tender age of 23) to find his sister, who went to Canada to spread the good word of the Quaker faith, but after marrying outside the Society of Friends and being rejected by that community, has disappeared.

Golding, William.
Rites of Passage. **1980.** Farrar. paper. 288pp. ISBN 0-374-52640-0.

Rendered in journal format, this metaphysical novel by an English Nobel laureate is literally an account, in rather stiff, formal prose, of a young British aristocrat's journey to New Zealand in the Napoleonic era, but the novel uses this one man's exposure to a wider universe as a paradigm of human obsession with and interpretation and internalization of new things greater than what one is accustomed to.

Moore, Susanna.
One Last Look. **2003.** Vintage. paper. 288pp. ISBN 1-4000-7541-6.

Moore takes a deliberate, even luxurious, look at the early years of the nineteenth century and, in diary format, records the observations, experiences, opinions, and attitudes of an Englishwoman sailing out to India with her sister and brother, the latter having been appointed Governor-General. In the course of a half-dozen years of the woman's residence in the exotic, dazzling subcontinent, Moore follows her deteriorating sense of superiority as she encounters and comes to appreciate the depths of the indigenous culture.

Phillips, Arthur.
The Egyptologist. **2004.** Random. 432pp. ISBN 1-4000-6250-0.

The author's flair for creative invention sits at the heart of this intriguing novel exploring ancient Egypt by way of a series of letters and journal entries composed by several narrators, Egyptologist Ralph Trilipush being the primary one. (Ralph leads a fictitious expedition to discover a pharaonic tomb in 1922.) The point is, though, that the narrative we are reading, including what Ralph tells us, is not necessarily the truth, and the fun of the novel is to discover what is true from what is *not*.

Descriptive—Highly Detailed

Good historical novelists have a knack for using language as a strong tool to describe place and character and to make details come alive. The following stories, embroidered with lavish details about places, times, and characters, immerse the reader in their almost palpable historical milieus.

Dunnett, Dorothy.
Niccolo Rising. **1986.** Vintage. paper. 496pp. ISBN 0-375-70477-9.

Dunnett is one of the most popular and critically regarded modern historical novelists, and one of her compelling cycles of interrelated novels is the House of Niccolo series, of which this title is the first volume (followed by six others). Time and place in this initial installment, as the story opens, is fifteenth-century Bruge. Agreeably engaged in a richly appointed adventure, the reader follows the exploits of a clumsy teenage dyer's apprentice morphing into the merchant-mathematician Nicholas vander Poele.

Goldman, Francisco.
The Divine Husband. **2004.** Atlantic Monthly. 496pp. ISBN 0-87113-915-4.

Two girls grow to womanhood as novitiates in a convent in late-nineteenth-century Central America. One, the primary focus of this richly detailed (and, yes, episodic and digressive, but also definitive of Central American society) novel, has children out of wedlock, one of whom may have been fathered by the great Cuban poet Jose Martí (who actually did spend time in Guatemala).

Jones, Edward P.

The Known World. **2003.** HarperCollins/Amistad. 400pp. ISBN 0-06-055754-0; Amistad. paper. 400pp. ISBN 0-06-055755-9.

Winner of the Pulitzer Prize and the National Book Critics Circle Award and short-listed for the National Book Award, this well-regarded novel—morally deep and complex in plot structure—is an extremely sensitive and atmospheric depiction, set in rural Virginia two decades before the outbreak of the Civil War, of a situation infrequently mined either in fiction or nonfiction: black slaveholders in the antebellum South. Many characters appear, each well defined, and the picture the author paints is wrought in substantial and perfect detail.

Mailer, Norman.

Ancient Evenings. **1983.** Warner. paper. 864pp. ISBN 0-446-35769-3.

Mailer is often accused of prolixity (especially upon the publication of this provocative novel), but here this American novelist of major standing visited the land of the pharaohs with exuberant results. Mailer's highly sensuous language evokes in no uncertain terms the accouterments and manners of ancient Egypt, in a rich panorama more graphic (violent, sexual) than most depictions of pharaonic Egypt. The culture and religion of that exciting-to-recall, ancient land arise from the author's copious research and highly tuned imagination.

McCullough, Colleen.

The Grass Crown. **1991.** Avon. paper. 1,077pp. ISBN 0-380-71082-X.

In her Masters of Rome series, focusing on Republican Rome, the era before Augustus wore the imperial crown, McCullough has carved out a successful niche. This novel (see also *Caesar* and *Caesar's Women*) pits Gauis Marius, conqueror of Germany, against his former friend and ally and now enemy, Lucius Cornelius Sulla, in a bloody, treacherous contest for power in Rome, relived here in all its high drama and gripping detail.

Vidal, Gore.

Empire. **1987.** Vintage. paper. 496pp. ISBN 0-375-70874-X.

In this novel (part of the author's American Chronicle series) about the United States in the post–Spanish-American War era—specifically, the country's entrée onto the stage of world powers—noted writer Vidal, considered one of the premier contemporary American historical novelists, trains his sharp and luxurious eye for descriptive detail on his twin concerns : power as exerted in the worlds of politics and journalism. The novel's electric polestar is fictional Caroline Sanford, granddaughter of Charlie Schuyler, a character who appeared previously in the series. Here, Caroline assumes control of a sleepy Washington, D.C., newspaper and makes it a political force to be reckoned with.

It's All in the Voice

Novels written in the way the characters would actually speak offer charm and allure—and authenticity.

Barlow, John.
Eating Mammals. **2004.** HarperPerennial. paper. 272pp. ISBN 0-06-059175-7.

In three linked novellas, the author employs regional dialect to depict the menacing but authentic-feeling atmosphere of a particular corner of late-nineteenth-century rural Yorkshire. Funny, supernatural, and brimming with highly evocative description, the trio of tales limns the lives of strange but compelling characters.

Cable, George Washington.
The Grandissimes. **1880.** Penguin. paper. 344pp. ISBN 0-14-043322-8.

This first novel by a New Orleans newspaper columnist and reporter maintains footing in both regionalism and romance as Cable portrays the customs and speech of Louisiana's Creole society (as well as Southern racial attitudes of the time). The plot centers on two lovers from feuding Creole families. The novel has secured its place as a classic of nineteenth-century regional literature that nevertheless transcends strictly regional interest.

Carey, Peter.
True History of the Kelly Gang. **2000.** Vintage. paper. 384pp. ISBN 0-37572467-2.

Australian Carey isn't especially known as a historical novelist, but simply as an outstanding one (and winner of the prestigious Booker Prize). This delightful, intelligent romp takes an entertaining position within an authentic historical setting, reconstructing in sprightly fashion the life and exploits of Ned Kelly, a late-nineteenth-century Australian author of mythic and heroic stature (sort of a Robin Hood to the ordinary folk in his defiance of colonial authority). Kelly writes down his own story, addressed to his infant daughter, in his hardly articulate but decidedly personal and electric style, with the rhythms and vocabulary of Australian English spoken by the uneducated, as he flees the police. (He will eventually be caught and hanged, in his mid-twenties.) He is viewed with great sympathy here for the hard, poverty-ridden life that drew him to desperate deeds, and his own voice is the most captivating aspect of the novel.

Edgeworth, Maria.

Castle Rackrent. **1800.** Oxford. paper. 176pp. ISBN 0-19-283563-7.

This slim novel is nevertheless a mighty effective depiction of a lost way of life. The admirably concise and technically brilliant novel takes the form of a memoir by a family retainer, related in the Irish dialect, who witnesses the fall of a dynasty of Irish gentry in the mid-eighteenth century. Observable through his loyalty to and fondness for his employer is the reality of the family's dissoluteness.

Hurston, Zora Neale.

Moses, Man of the Mountain. **1939.** Perennial. paper. 336pp. ISBN 0-06-091994-9.

Hurston, born in a small black community in central Florida, is one of the most resonant voices to emerge from the Harlem Renaissance, the black arts movement centered in New York City in the 1920s and 1930s. She wrote four novels. *Moses* was ostensibly a retelling of the Bible story, but it is imbued with the speech and tropes of black folklore, transcending its literal level to become a provocative allegory of the state of black America in her time.

Kennedy, William.

Legs. **1975.** Penguin. paper. 320pp. ISBN 0-14-006484-2.

This is the inaugural volume in Kennedy's ongoing, highly regarded, and vastly engrossing cycle of novels taking place in his native Albany, New York, in the criminal underworld of the 1920s, 1930s, and 1940s. *Legs* sets the stage beautifully, like a sturdy yet certainly visible and attractive platform upon which the entire sequence can rest, but the novel is a perfectly viable reading experience by itself. Here, Kennedy lends credence and even compassion to the life and career of real-life gangster Jack "Legs" Diamond. As careful as Kennedy's social description is, and as impressive as his acute recognition of how best to show a character, it is his prose style, so highly reflective of the place and time and how the characters speak and view the world, that resonates most in readers' minds. Kennedy's rough-and-tumble, street-wise language, amazingly eloquent in its unsophisticated sophistication, *is* the atmosphere.

Turner, Nancy E.

Sarah's Quilt: The Continuing Story of Sarah Agnes Prine, 1906. **2005.** St. Martin's/Thomas Dunne. 416pp. ISBN 0-312-33262-4.

This completely absorbing novel is a sequel to the author's equally riveting *These Is My Words* (see below). The story, featuring the same intrepid central character, Sarah Prine, moves up in time to the year 1906, but the setting, which is of paramount importance to the story, remains the same: the Arizona Territory. Struggles against nature dominate the lives of Sarah and her family, and in an authentic voice, she narrates their plights and triumphs.

Turner, Nancy E.
These Is My Words. **1998.** Regan. paper. 400pp. ISBN 0-06-098751-0.

Based on actual events in the life of the author's great-grandmother, this exciting, rivetingly detailed novel, composed as if it were a diary, follows the exploits of Sarah Price, who lived and exerted her strong personality in the rough Arizona Territory in the late 1880s. Sarah grows up determined, self-educated, and passionate, and her love for a cavalry officer survives separation. What sparkles most in this novel is Sarah's voice and how it matures in style and eloquence as she gains wisdom and grace with the passing years.

Almost Archaic

These novels are written in a rather formal style representing the way people used to write, not necessarily how they spoke.

Brooks, Geraldine.
March. **2005.** Viking. 280pp. ISBN 0-670-03335-9.

With creativity and élan, Brooks imagines a life for Captain March, the father in Louisa May Alcott's classic novel *Little Women*, basing him on Alcott's own father, Branson Alcott. In formal language reflective of more formal times, it brings to beautiful life Civil War–era America.

Busch, Frederick.
The Night Inspector. **1999.** Ballantine. paper. 278pp. ISBN 0-449-00615-8.

Manhattan immediately following the Civil War provides an atmospheric setting for this highly esteemed literary writer's novel about a disfigured army veteran. It narrates his story as he partners with a now-down-and-out Herman Melville in an attempt to rescue a group of black children from what is basically still a slave situation. Period detail—of New York City's dark, seamy underside—brings the story to life, but the real electrifying agent here is the beautiful language, matching the stylistic flourishes with which people wrote and spoke at the time.

Gregory, Patrick.
The Daguerreotype. **2004.** Syracuse University. 256pp. ISBN 0-8156-0825-X.

Elizabeth Gow is a young Englishwoman who accompanies her scholar father to America to make a better life. Over the course of the novel—1849 to 1929—she becomes a woman *and* an American. Written in rich, deliberate prose deeply evocative of the writing style of the period.

Martin, Valerie.
Mary Reilly. **1990.** Vintage. paper. 263pp. ISBN 0-375-72599-7.

In her own lower-class, uneducated voice, brandishing her own simple eloquence, a maid in the household of Dr. Henry Jekyll of Edinburgh, Scotland, recounts her observations as her employer sinks deeper into madness. This very imaginative take on Robert Louis Stevenson's classic tale *Dr. Jekyll and Mr. Hyde* is at once psychologically rigorous and as page-turning as the best horror story.

Miles, Rosalind.
I, Elizabeth. **1994.** Three Rivers. paper. 656pp. ISBN 0-609-80910-5.

In a crowded field of novels about Elizabeth I of England, this one ranks near the top. Elizabeth inherited a country deeply riven by religion and at odds with the powers of Europe, but upon her death 45 years later, she left to her Stuart successor a rich, united, powerful kingdom. By having the great queen narrate her own story, in a voice she would have used, Miles finds the person behind the politics, the true being behind the image; the result is an understanding of power politics at a time when it was practiced as an art form, and of a woman whose heart was broken in her relationships with men but whose true love was the throne of England—and retaining occupancy of it.

Peachmont, Christopher.
The Green and Gold: A Novel of Andrew Marvell: Spy, Politician, Poet. **2004.** St. Martin's/Thomas Dunne. 384pp. ISBN 0-312-31450-7.

The subtitle pretty much sums up the life and career of the seventeenth-century English adventurer known, most famously, as the author of the beautiful poem "To His Coy Mistress." Executed in a prose style derived from that time period, this exciting novel, rendered as an autobiography, imagines details about a man who served as a secret agent for the Puritan dictator Oliver Cromwell.

Settle, Mary Lee.
I, Roger Williams. **2001.** Norton. paper. 320pp. ISBN 0-393-32383-8.

This distinguished American novelist has Roger Williams, the founder of Rhode Island, recapitulating the events of his life from the vantage point of old age. An immigrant from England to *New* England, Williams discovers the Puritan church in Massachusetts is not to his liking; he is eventually banished. An imaginative reconstruction of a major early American figure, wrought in language appropriate to the times.

Settle, Mary Lee.
Prisons. **1973.** University of South Carolina. paper. 235pp. ISBN 1-57003-114-2.

Published third in the author's landmark <u>Beulah Quintet</u> sequence of novels, *Prisons* actually is the first volume in terms of the time period and family chronology covered by the set. It takes place in seventeenth-century England and is narrated by young soldier Johnny Church, speaking in the rich (and somewhat archaic to contemporary ears) language of the time. (Johnny's illegitimate child, fathered when he was still a teenager, is apparently the ancestor of the Virginia pioneers Settle writes about in *O Beulah Land*). Vividly re-created here are the labyrinthine English politics of the day, namely the Civil Wars, which resulted in the execution of King Charles I and the (temporary) abolition of the monarchy.

Dreamy

The language in these novels evokes a kind of illusory feeling, almost like dreaming.

Antunes, António Lobo.
The Inquisitors' Manual. **2002.** Grove. paper. 435pp. ISBN 0-8021-4052-1.

> The author, who is Portuguese, has achieved substantial international renown, and readers who avail themselves of this magnificent novel will completely understand the basis of his fame. The main character, Senhor Francisco, is a minister in the government of Portugal's infamous dictator, António de Salazar, but has been incapacitated by a stroke. Through Francisco's elusive stream of consciousness, as well as the consciousness of several other characters, the reader witnesses the effects of state tyranny on a personal level.

Baricco, Alessandro.
Silk. **1997.** Vintage. paper. 91pp. ISBN 0-375-70382-9.

> An international best seller, this Italian author's astonishingly beautiful and haunting novel is set in France and Japan in the 1860s. A French silk-worm trader takes a business trip to Japan and becomes obsessed with the mistress of a local warlord. The format is a series of very brief chapters, written in seductively spare language. This short, swift novel is as wise as a fable, as poignant as a fairy tale, and as fragile as a dream.

Chatwin, Bruce.
The Viceroy of Ouidah. **1980.** Penguin. paper. 155pp. ISBN 0-14-011290-1.

> A family in Africa, grown rich in the nineteenth century from the slave trade to the New World, declines in wealth and privilege: this is the basic premise of this distinguished and much-loved English novelist's poignant novella. Chatwin is known as a master stylist, and this narrative should be read for its language alone, but ultimately its allure is that it is as illusory as a fantasy: Place, character, and storyline are all enigmatic, founded on a chimera.

Delaney, Frank.

Ireland. **2005.** HarperCollins. 576pp. ISBN 0-06-056348-6.

This is as big a novel as Ireland is small as a country, but both are mighty. The novel has as great an impact despite its flab-risking length as Ireland has on the world despite its geographical limitations. The history of Ireland comes to the fore in its high drama and heroism by way of a storyteller, who in 1951 visits the home of little Ronan O'Mara, who exchanges yarns about Irish history for food. Eventually the intrigued Ronan grows up and becomes a storyteller himself. The history of a place is given personalization in the life of Ronan, and the implicit "duty" of historical fiction is achieved here.

Ducornet, Rikki.

Gazelle. **2003.** Knopf. 208pp. ISBN 0-375-41124-0; Anchor. paper. 189pp. ISBN 0-385-72043-2.

A 13-year-old American girl, daughter of a history professor, awakens not only to the steamy sensuality of 1950s Cairo but also to her own sexuality as, more or less left by her parents to her own devices, she finds a home-away-from-home in the shop of a master perfumer, who teaches her about the magical arts of the past.

Hand, Elizabeth.

Mortal Love. **2004.** Morrow. 320pp. ISBN 0-06-105171-5.

Hand deftly spirits the reader back and forth in time, from the early 1880s to contemporary times, in a richly presented novel set in London and featuring a young American painter (in the chapters focused on the past) and an American critic writing a book on Tristan and Iseult (in those chapters illuminating the present). A woman with auburn hair is the connection between the two men and the two time periods; the result is a delightful, convincing depiction of obsession and fantasy.

Hodgson, Barbara.

The Lives of Shadows. **2004.** Chronicle. 185pp. ISBN 0-8118-3926-5.

This mysterious, even ghostly, novel, gorgeously illustrated with photographs, clippings, drawings, maps, and floor plans, evokes in polished prose the Damascus (Syria) of the pre–World War II years. The plot centers on a young British man who, in 1914, visits the Middle East and is compelled by his love of the surroundings to buy a house in Damascus. The history of his house's ownership becomes a stunning exploration of lost worlds and individuals.

Ondaatje, Michael.

The English Patient. **1992.** Vintage. paper. 320pp. ISBN 0-676-51420-0.

Winner of Britain's prestigious Booker Prize (for a novel written in English and published in Great Britain, Ireland, and the Commonwealth), this novel by a highly respected Canadian writer was translated into a successful movie. (The book remains superior to the movie in depth and resonance.) In a villa in Italy, as World War II finally draws to a close, a Canadian nurse continues to care for a wounded British soldier who remembers little about himself. They are joined in the abandoned hospital by two other equally fascinating characters, leaving the reader with a haunting, even hallucinatory, exploration of personal psychology battered by the individual horrors of war.

All About Me: Fictional Autobiography

Did these people really write their own life stories? These novels certainly read as if they did. Through these stories, the reader is treated to up-close-and-personal viewpoints on topics ranging from Japanese geisha culture to life on the American prairie.

Berger, Thomas.
Little Big Man. **1964.** Delta. paper. 480pp. ISBN 0-385-29829-3.

> Berger is known for his satire and even outright comedy as he limns common lives caught up in the foolishness and ludicrousness of modern culture. In this particular novel, made into a popular movie starring Dustin Hoffman, the author quietly build ups a farcical situation that on the exterior seems realistic. It is the story of 111-year-old Jack Crabb, who has lived as both an Indian and a white man—the only white survivor of the Battle of Little Big Horn—as well as a gunfighter and con artist. Crabb's reminiscences define the term *hyperbole*, yet the novel overall is a marvelous re-creation of life on the prairie in the mid- and late nineteenth century.

Elyot, Amanda.
The Memoirs of Helen of Troy. **2005.** Crown. paper. 320pp. ISBN 0-307-20998-9.

> The infamous beauty, Helen of Troy, whose comely face launched a thousand ships, pens her memoirs for her daughter, Hermione, to tell how she became such a legendary figure. Her story is one of deciding to listen to the heart's voice rather than the mind's (although she certainly comes across here as an intelligent person—but also self-centered and self-righteous) as Helen grew up in Sparta, the half-immortal daughter of Zeus by Leda, the Spartan queen. She was kidnapped and made a woman by Theseus, king of Athens, and by the time she married Menelaus, brother of Agamemnon, Helen was quite aware that her beauty not only aroused jealousy but also could be used for manipulation. When she fled to Troy with the handsome, exciting Paris—well, we all know about the Trojan War. A sparkling conjoining of history and mythology.

George, Margaret.
The Autobiography of Henry VIII; with Notes by His Fool, Will Somers. **1986.**
St. Martin's/Griffin. paper. 944pp. ISBN 0-312-19439-0.

George specializes in highly detailed, fictional biographies of famous historical figures, and in this instance she tackles the much-written-about Tudor king of England. The premise here is that Henry himself is getting his own story down, his memoir interspersed—spiced—with commentary from the court jester, who knew his master well. An intimate picture of a flawed but extremely significant personality, in whose hands rested considerable power.

Golden, Arthur.
Memoirs of a Geisha. **1997.** Knopf. 448pp. ISBN 0-375-40011-7; Vintage. paper. 434pp. ISBN 0-679-78158-7.

A poignant and extremely informative fictional autobiography of a famous Japanese geisha, trained to please men. Born in 1929 in a fishing village, she was sold by her poor father into that station in life as a nine-year-old girl. Her career is based in the ancient capital of Kyoto, and her education in the elaborate world of service in the geisha house is a fascinating history lesson for contemporary readers. But with the advent of World War II, her role in life is by necessity changed, into one of her own making.

Graves, Robert.
I, Claudius. **1934.** Vintage. paper. 480pp. ISBN 0-679-7247-X.
Claudius the God. **1934.** Vintage. paper. 546pp. ISBN 0-679-72573-3.

Esteemed British fiction writer Graves ushers the reader deeply into the history of ancient Rome with this two-part fictionalized autobiography of the retiring scholar-emperor Claudius, who succeeded his murdered nephew, Caligula, on the imperial throne. Vivid scenes and equally vibrant characterizations distinguish these two highly accurate novels. The labyrinthine, Byzantine politics of ancient Rome—especially how certain men gained and then lost the imperial throne—is a difficult path for the reader to follow in many other sources, here made comprehensible and compelling by Graves.

Kohn, Rebecca.
The Gilded Chamber. **2004.** Rugged Land; dist. by St. Martin's. 320pp. ISBN 1-59071-024-X.

This novel about Jewish heroine Esther (the subject of the Old Testament *Book of Esther*), an orphaned child who rose to become the queen of the Persian empire, is both psychologically penetrating and elegantly and sensuously written—to say nothing of historically true to the times. Esther, narrating her own story, is rendered in three dimensions, as a strong, wise character who could take advantage of Persian King Xerxes for the good of her Jewish people.

Pressfield, Steven.

The Virtues of War. **2004.** Doubleday. 368pp. ISBN 0-385-50099-8.

The enigmatic but highly alluring Alexander the Great, king of Macedonia and conqueror of the known world at what is considered these days quite a tender age, supplies endlessly exciting fodder for the historical novelist. An experienced practitioner, Pressfield imparts to the king a marvelously effective voice in relating his own exploits. Details are immaculate—particularly those of battle scenes—as is the insight provided into Alexander's complex mind.

Yourcenar, Marguerite.

Memoirs of Hadrian. **1951.** Noonday. paper. 408pp. ISBN 0-374-50348-6.

From a French writer of extremely precise prose, this is an elegant and eloquent explication of the complicated character of Rome's Emperor Hadrian as well as the times that shaped him and to which he himself gave shape. The premise of this seminal work in the history and development of the historical novel, rightly regarded as a classic in the field, is that Hadrian looks back from the vantage of old age over his dramatic life. This becoming-one-with-a-historical-figure, writing about a person from the past from the inside out, is a great challenge for a novelist, and Yourcenar's novel is one of the best of the type.

Poetic, Spare Language

Following is a selection of novels written as if they were prose poems; that is, tightly textured, and all the more effective for it.

Barrico, Alessandro.

Without Blood. **2004.** Knopf. 112pp. ISBN 1-4000-4145-7.

The novels of this award-winning Italian writer (which include the lovely *Silk*) are indeed like prose poems: sparely and impressionistically written. In this one, he observes the personal effects of an unnamed country's civil war on two individuals on opposite sides, at two points in time: many years ago when the war was winding down, and now, when the two antagonists are old.

Blackwell, Elise.

Hunger. **2003.** Back Bay. paper. 132pp. ISBN 0-316-90719-7.

The novel's title is exactly what the citizens of Leningrad faced during the long weeks and months of siege by the German army in World War II. In precise, concise, beautifully clear language, the survival choices and strategies are exquisitely yet searingly explored. This is a perfect case of the tighter the better, to create a more graphic impression on the reader.

Ephron, Amy.
White Rose: Una Rosa Blanca. **1999.** Ballantine. paper. 288pp. ISBN 0-345-44110-9.

This is an elegantly styled but nevertheless vibrant and even pulsing novel based on the true story of Evangelina Cisneros, teenage daughter of a Cuban revolutionary, who was imprisoned for purported revolutionary activities in Havana in 1897, at the height of the island's struggle for freedom from Spain. A reporter for William Randolph Hearst's newspaper is sent ostensibly to interview her but actually to effect her rescue and escape to America. Love between the two inevitably springs up.

Maxwell, William.
The Folded Leaf. **1945.** Vintage. paper. 289pp. ISBN 0-679-77256-1.

Set in Maxwell's native Illinois in the 1920s (he was the distinguished and much-loved fiction editor at the *New Yorker* for many years, and his hometown of Lincoln, Illinois, supplies an important backdrop to his own fiction), this novel charts the history of a friendship between two dissimilar boys, from high school to college, until an outside factor comes between them. Written in this author's trademark direct, clear, consummately articulate style. (See his *So Long, See You Tomorrow* for further evidence of how extremely effective Maxwell's strong, understated prose is.)

Otsuka, Julie.
When the Emperor Was Divine. **2002.** Knopf. paper. 160pp. ISBN 0-385-72181-1.

In just a handful of chapters constructed from precise, never excessive detail, the author's succinct, indelible prose is the perfect medium for telling a sobering story of one family's victimization in what is now considered a national disgrace: the post–Pearl Harbor internment of thousands of Japanese Americans, displaced from their homes along the Pacific coast, to camps much farther inland for "national security" reasons. Like a stiletto blade in her sheer, clean slicing, the author relates what one family endured during their imprisonment and what they had to deal with after their release: continued prejudice from the non-Asian community and their own physical and mental deterioration. The spare language contributes significantly to the novel's poignancy.

Rubens, Bernice.
The Sergeant's Tale. 2005. Abacus; dist. by Trafalgar Square. 224pp. ISBN 0-349-11730-6.

The setting is British Mandate Palestine in 1947, and the author, basing this precisely styled, psychologically profound, emotionally gripping novel on a real incident, uses the kidnapping of two British officers by a Jewish resistance movement to show the many sides and interests at play in the establishment of an independent Jewish state. The novel has resonance and meaning for today's terrorist climate in the area.

Yourcenar, Marguerite.
Coup de Grâce. **1939.** Farrar. paper. 164pp. ISBN 0-374-51631-6.

   Set in the Baltic region of Europe just after World War I, and written by a well-respected French novelist, this stylish novel—its elegant, precise language nevertheless bespeaking great passions and emotions—relates the effects of a love triangle on its participants: a Prussian fighting on the White Russian side against the Bolsheviks, his long-time best friend, and the woman who loves the friend.

Confessional

Boy, have I got a story to tell you. . . .

Allende, Isabel.
Zorro. 2005. HarperCollins. 392pp. ISBN 0-06-077897-0.

   Yes, *the* Zorro! The masked avenger from popular lore, the Robin Hood of colonial California, is given a boyhood and adolescence in this novel by avidly read Latin American (now a resident of California) Allende, who tells the tale of Diego de la Vega, from his mixed-blood family background to his education in Spain (where he assumed the name of Zorro and began his fight for justice), in the form of a "tell-all" testimony by—well, the reader does not discover the identity of the narrator until the novel's end, and the ending won't be spoiled here!

Drabble, Margaret.
The Red Queen. **2004.** Harcourt. 368pp. ISBN 0-15-101106-0.

   Highly respected British novelist Drabble typically writes extremely thoughtful domestic dramas as well as investigations into real lives behind reputations in academe, and this novel actually fits the mold: a bilevel retelling of the life of an eighteenth-century Korean crown princess, narrating her portion of the story, and an academic who, reading the princess's memoirs on her way to a conference in Korea, identifies parallels between her life and the princess's.

Eco, Umberto.
Baudolino. **2002.** Harcourt. 528pp. ISBN 0-15-100690-3; Harvest. paper. 544pp. ISBN 0-15-602906-5.

   The fictional flair of this Italian professor of semiotics was brought to the world's attention by his international best seller, *The Name of the Rose*. In this later novel, the Byzantine capital of Constantinople is under siege by the knights of the Fourth Crusade in the early years of the thirteenth century. A man by the name of Baudolino saves a historian and high court official, to whom he tells his life story, particularly how, as a boy in Italy, he was "adopted" by the great Holy Roman Emperor Frederick Barbarossa. Adventure is mixed with erudite discussions of theology, government, language, geography, and politics; the ultimate question this provocative novel advances is: Where lies actual truth in documented history?

Gaines, Ernest.

The Autobiography of Miss Jane Pittman. **1971.** Bantam. paper. 272pp. ISBN 0-553-26357-9.

Gaines's famous novel takes the form of the memoirs of a 110-year-old ex-slave, remembering into a tape recorder the chain of events that marked her long life, from the late Civil War to the civil rights movement of the 1960s. A character of great strength, fortitude, and accumulated wisdom, whom Gaines develops with both the subtle accuracy of gesture and identifying inner force of a master sculptor, Miss Jane tells an amazing story that is both unique to her experience and encapsulates the black American experience.

Healey, Judith Koll.

The Canterbury Papers. **2003.** HarperPerennial. paper. 353pp. ISBN 0-06-052535-5.

The twelfth-century Alois, whom the author refers to as the "forgotten princess of France," is here given a full-fledged and even exciting life story. Alois, of the royal house of France, was stepdaughter of the famous English queen Eleanor of Aquitaine, and in this highly dramatic narrative, she recounts a mesmerizing, mysterious mission in which she takes part: to secure a cache of letters the queen wrote and now wants back.

Mailer, Norman.

The Gospel According to the Son. **1997.** Ballantine. paper. 256pp. ISBN 0-345-43408-0.

There's little doubt from the title what this novel is about: the gospel told by Christ himself; in other words, his "memoir." And Mailer's provocative, clever, often verbose treatment imbues a difficult historical character to humanize with all-too-recognizably human qualities and attitudes— in other words, believability. Christ worries about his celebrity and miracle making; he is disturbed that his Father in Heaven is so uncommunicative. Given Mailer's reputation for prolixity, verbal flamboyance, and barely concealed egotism, this is a more straightforward narrative than is usually expected of him, and is certainly less reflective of his own untrammeled, all-about-me personality.

Maxwell, William.

So Long, See You Tomorrow. **1980.** Random. paper. 144pp. ISBN 0-679-76720-7.

This National Book Award winner, by the longtime, beloved fiction editor at the *New Yorker*, is at once lovely and electric in its concision: as lean as poetry and as tough as a diamond. The effects of a murder and suicide in Lincoln, Illinois (Maxwell's hometown) in the 1920s are recalled by the narrator 50 years later, because his involvement in what happened altered his life forever.

Robinson, Marilynne.

Gilead. 2004. Farrar. 256pp. ISBN 0-374-15389-2.

Robinson's highly anticipated second novel, which appeared more than 20 years after the publication of her well-regarded first one, *Housekeeping*, is a historical novel, although never actually billed as such. In tight, rigorous, poetic prose, the author tells the story through a 77-year-old preacher in Iowa in 1956. He recalls for his young son the pre–Civil War abolitionist activities of his grandfather, in conflict with the pacifist ideals of his father.

Chapter 5

Mood and Atmosphere

The exact feel of foggy old London, finding humor in the retelling of biblical stories, the precarious state of the ancient Egyptian state under a weak line of pharaohs, a fairy tale-esque excursion back to colonial Mississippi, and great romantic entanglements: The situations that conjure up a certain mood and atmosphere in a historical novel are endless. If that is the writer's intent and strong suit, the mood a novel can put the reader in, or the atmosphere in which the writer can envelope the reader, is palpable from the first page in a well-written historical novel. Consequently, mood and atmosphere make up a strong factor attracting a reader to a particular novel, a novel in which, say, you feel as if you are in another world or that forces you onto the edge of your seat with its unflagging suspense, or one that irresistibly makes you chuckle at the sarcasm or slapstick; take your pick of the ways to "feel" a novel.

This grouping of historical fiction is actually one of the most exciting and creative in establishing linking themes from one novel to another. After all, we all like a mood to reach out and touch our senses, and then to keep going.

Flights of Fantasy

Elements of unreality can contribute considerable spice to a historical novel.

Adrian, Christine.
Gob's Grief. **2001.** Vintage. paper. 400pp. ISBN 0-375-72624-1.

In 1863, Gob Woodhall's twin brother, a Union soldier, is killed, and in the years following the Civil War, Gob's grief is so intense and unrelenting that he devises a machine to bring his brother and all the other war dead back to life. History (and real historical figures) converges with fantasy in this mesmerizing tale about the catastrophe of war.

Branston, Julian.
Tilting at Windmills: A Novel of Cervantes and the Errant Knight. **2005.** Crown. 320pp. ISBN 1-4000-4928-8.

This highly creative work imagines the provenance of Cervantes's masterpiece, *Don Quixote*; we witness the great Spanish poet composing his seminal narrative despite great obstacles, including falling in love with a beautiful duchess who rejects him, and a fellow poet who is out to get him. But who comes to his aid is none other than his own creation, Don Quixote. A colorful blend of fact, fiction, and fantasy.

Clarke, Susannah.
Jonathan Strange & Mr. Norrell. **2004.** Bloomsbury. 800pp. ISBN 1-58234-416-7.

A long, elaborate, and agreeably fanciful first novel that re-creates with both great detail and an authoritative voice the Britain of the early nineteenth century, more specifically, the community of English magicians at that time. Magic, so its seems, has fallen out of practice; magicians want only to *speak* of it, not *do* it. But conditions come about that jerk magic out of its hibernation. An absolutely charming mixture of history and fantasy, this novel was critically acclaimed upon its release, and deservedly so.

Sherwood, Frances.
The Book of Splendor. **2002.** Norton. 352pp. ISBN 0-393-02138-6; Norton. paper. 352pp. ISBN 0-393-32458-3.

Any potential or past visitors to the gorgeous city of Prague should relish this novel set in the Czech capital in the seventeenth century. From the Jewish quarter, where two lovers (one of whom is the infamous golem, created from mud) attempt a forbidden relationship, to the inner sanctums of the castle, where the Hapsburg emperor Rudolph II resides in his obsession with immortality, the author creates a palpable atmosphere of adventure, romance, and mysticism.

Walpole, Horace.
The Castle of Otranto. **1764.** Oxford. paper. 176pp. ISBN 0-19-283440-1.

With delicious gothic overtones, Walpole takes the reader to twelfth-century Italy, to the castle of the Prince of Otranto, and the ongoing struggle over who is the right and true prince involves a giant and a sword with miraculous power. This is a much more sophisticated treatment than a brief description might suggest; in other words, a tale for readers of literary fiction.

Welty, Eudora.
The Robber Bridegroom. **1942.** Harcourt. paper. 185pp. ISBN 0-15-676807-0.

This first novel by one of the preeminent Southern writers of the twentieth century (best known for her lyrical short stories), is a mesmerizing fictional journey into colonial Mississippi. Welty tells the dark but delightful, fairy tale-esque yarn of bandit Jamie Lockhart, who absconds with Rosamund, daughter of a pioneer planter.

Great Romances

What is there to say? There's nothing like a novel that sets up a romantic mood.

Audourard, Antoine.
Farewell, My Only One: A Novel of Abelard and Heloise. **2004.** Houghton. 336pp. ISBN 0-618-15286-5.

A beautiful take on the legendary (but historically real) romance between Peter Abelard, a twelfth-century French theologian and teacher, and Heloise, the well-educated niece of the canon of Notre Dame Cathedral, whom Abelard serves as tutor. This author's spin on the story is to have it told by Abelard's clerk, who is also in love with Heloise.

Byatt, A. S.
Possession: A Romance. **1990.** Vintage. paper. 576pp. ISBN 0-679-73590-9.

Winner of the prestigious Booker Prize (for best novel written in English in Britain, Ireland, and the Commonwealth), Byatt's intricate and sumptuous novel, written in her trademark dense prose style, absorbs readers in its dual, parallel storylines. Two contemporary scholars, female and male, find mutual attraction while researching the lives of two Victorian poets, also female and male, who, the scholars discover, were involved in an extramarital affair.

Dandicat, Edwidge.
The Farming of Bones. **1998.** Penguin. paper. 320pp. ISBN 0-14-028049-9.

A love story set amid swirling social and political horrors of the outside world that have a decided effect on the lovers' personal lives is always a provocative formula for a compelling historical novel. Dandicat takes this timeless theme and sets it in an authentic historical situation that will be new territory for almost all American fiction readers: the oppressive days of the Trujillo dictatorship in the Dominican Republic. In the 1930s, the Dominican caudillo ended the existing mutuality between the Republic and neighboring Haiti by calling for the eradication of Haitians living within Dominican borders. Anabelle and Sebastien are at risk of persecution, and in old age she remembers the tragedy of "ethnic cleansing." She records her years-long search for the lost Sebastien. To read Dandicat's rich, vivid prose is to ache at love's separation and life's resilience.

Fowles, John.
The French Lieutenant's Woman. **1969.** Back Bay. paper. 480pp. ISBN 0-316-29116-1.

A brilliant, cerebral, but at the same time breathtakingly sensual juxtaposition of a contemporary romance (set in England at the time the novel was written) and a Victorian one—the much richer and compelling of the two storylines—between an amateur paleontologist and a social outcast, purportedly the jilted lover of a French naval officer. The parallels and contrasts between sexuality then and now form the thematic thread.

Frazier, Charles.
Cold Mountain. **1997.** Vintage. paper. 449pp. ISBN 0-375-70075-7.

This National Book Award winner started it all; that is, it ushered in the current renaissance of literary historical fiction, particularly the recognition of historical fiction's as a highly commercial commodity by the publishing industry, as compelling reading by the general reading public, and as serious art by critics. A sumptuous, exciting updating of the Ulysses tale, in this novel a Confederate soldier, AWOL from the front, is on a long return, by foot, to his North Carolina home and the woman he loves but hardly had time to get to know before marching off to war.

Hazard, Shirley.
The Great Fire. **2003.** Farrar. 288pp. ISBN 0-374-27821-0; Picador. paper. 336 pp. ISBN 0-312-42358-6.

Hazard is a highly regarded Australian fiction writer, and she returned to the world's literary stage in 2003, after an absence of 20 years, with a critical and popular smash. The title refers to the destruction of World War II; the time is 1947, the scene is war-ravaged East Asia. The hero of the novel is a young Englishman who is part of the Allied Occupation Forces, surveying the specifics of war damage. He meets the teenage daughter of a local Australian commander, and a beautiful, quite touching love story unfolds.

Hergesheimer, Joseph.
Java Head. **1919.** Kessinger. paper. 346pp. ISBN 1-4179-1822-5.

This generally forgotten American novelist wrote a lasting, even classic, novel that continues to hold up both as a compelling narrative and a good example of the historical novel. It is set in the port city of Salem, Massachusetts, in the 1840s, during the exciting era of the clipper ship, one of the high points of American dominance of the oceans. Each chapter of the novel is written from the point of view of a different character; in this way the author captures that romantic time by juxtaposing not only individual stories but also the contrast of cultures. The plot centers on the late return home of the *Nautilus;* when it finally sails into port, the young captain has with him a surprise: his new Chinese bride. But he had left his true love interest at home, and his interest is rekindled—and he soon regrets his marriage.

Langley, Lee.
Distant Music. **2003.** Milkweed. 332pp. ISBN 1-57131-040-1.

In this imaginative use of history, two Portuguese lovers, one Catholic and the other Jewish, surface first in Madeira in 1429, then are reincarnated in Faro in 1489, Lisbon in 1855, and London in 2000. A romantic and deeply atmospheric tale of love conquering all, with Portugal's dramatic history as an exciting and then former world power as its backdrop.

May, John.
Poe and Fanny. **2004.** Algonquin. 320pp. ISBN 1-56512-427-8.

May imagines a love affair, in the year 1844, between the 36-year-old writer Edgar Allan Poe, living in New York City, at the apogee of his fame and creativity but nevertheless struggling to make ends meet, and the real-life Fanny Osgood, who was also famous at that time (but is now a name lost in obscurity). The author's staging of the relationship between Poe, beset by personal demons, and Fanny, separated from her husband, has as its colorfully backdrop details of pre–Civil War New York, but the nature of the couple's feelings commands the reader's primary attention.

Mitchell, Judith Claire.
The Last Day of the War. **2004.** Pantheon. 384pp. ISBN 0-375-42166-1.

At the termination of World War I, a clandestine organization called Erinyes works to avenge Turkey's massacre of Armenians in 1915. In St. Louis, an 18-year-old Jewish girl falls in love with an Armenian-American soldier and follows him to Paris. He is involved in Erinyes, whose cause she adopts.

Sontag, Susan.
The Volcano Lover. **1992.** Picador. paper. 432pp. ISBN 0-312-42007-2.

Sontag was known for her intellectual investigations and philosophizing in essay form, but she was also a formidable, resonant fiction writer, as evidenced by this lushly detailed novel about the great historical love triangle involving Sir William Hamilton, the British ambassador to the Kingdom of the Two Sicilies in the late eighteenth century and collector of antiquities; his wife, Emma; and her lover, the great heroic admiral, Lord Nelson. Passion is explored within a larger context of ideas: social conventions, the status of women, and the darker sides of collecting art.

In the Head: The Psychology of War

War, of course, does its damage to the mind as well as to the body and personal property. These are powerful explorations of the tragedies that fall under war's long shadow.

Barker, Pat.
The Ghost Road. **1995.** Plume. paper. 278pp. ISBN 0-452-27672-1.
This deeply gripping novel brings to a close Barker's celebrated World War I trilogy, which began with *Regeneration* and continued with *The Eye in the Door*. These are not battlefield depictions, but rather explorations of the consequences of the dreadful trench warfare of World War I—specifically, treating shell-shocked British soldiers to enable them to return to service. As the war draws to a close in this final installment in the trilogy, the country is depleted of young men and its citizenry is exhausted from the fight.

Edmunds, Walter D.
Drums along the Mohawk. **1936.** Syracuse. paper. 688pp. ISBN 0-815-60457-2.
Yet another novel about the Revolutionary War, this one distinguishes itself by its realism—the tone of romantic adventure with which many Revolutionary War novels are imbued is absent—as it trains a revealing light on the individuals living in New York State's Mohawk Valley and the impact the war has on ordinary lives.

Flanagan, Thomas.
The Year of the French. **1979.** Maple Tree Press. paper. 648pp. ISBN 1-59017-108-X.
This sweeping epic centers on an actual historical event: the landing of a French military force in Ireland in 1798, ostensibly to aid the Irish in throwing off British rule. Told from diverse perspectives, from the French general to a local poet to a Protestant landowner, the narrative is beautifully written, moves along rapidly, and, most important, captures perfectly the troubled time and place as personally experienced.

Keneally, Thomas.
Gossip from the Front. **1975.** Harvest. paper. 228pp. ISBN 0-15-636469-7.
In 1918, as World War I drags on unmercifully and each day soldiers die by the thousands, and each side is firmly entrenched in its trenches, a group meets in a railroad car in the forests of France to negotiate a peace. Each negotiator carries his own personal agenda and prejudices as he faces the enemy that seems, at this point, unbeatable. An extremely thoughtful and tension-filled novel about the effects of personalities on the course of war.

Oran, Michael B.
Reunion. **2003.** Plume. paper. 353pp. ISBN 0-452-28514-3.

> For diverse personal reasons, the surviving members of an American battalion that fought in the Battle of the Bulge in World War II reconvene 50 years after the event in the Belgium village where they fought. This first novel excels at making clear the psychology of such a confrontation with one's wartime past, as in an almost thriller-like fashion the battalion's long-held secrets are revealed.

Unsworth, Barry.
The Songs of the Kings. **2003.** Norton. paper. 342pp. ISBN 0-393-32283-1.

> Greek king Agamemnon has assembled a mighty fleet for his upcoming attack on Troy, which is prompted by Paris's kidnapping of Agamemnon's brother's wife, the lovely Helen. But the king must do something about the winds that are keeping his fleet from crossing the Aegean Sea. An excellent depiction of the psychology of classical mentality, particularly regarding war and Agamemnon's desire to maintain his coalition and thus his power.

Yarbrough, Steve.
Prisoners of War. **2004.** Vintage. paper. 304pp. ISBN 1-4000-3062-5.

> World War II is two years away from its conclusion, and its consequences are now affecting even the small Mississippi farming town of Loring: There is a German POW contingency working in the local cotton fields. But teenager Don Timms views the great conflagration consuming Europe in his own strictly personal terms: his release from the tedium of his hometown and the bad associations it has for him (primarily, and understandably, the recent suicide of his father and his mother's wayward ways). He plans to enlist once he turns 18. Teenage angst, usual in anyone, is compounded here—and described by Yarbrough in clear, concise prose—by an extra layer of family trouble: The main character has to face his community's deeply entrenched racism (his friend L.C. is black), and there are local echoes of the current dysfunction the whole world is experiencing.

Nostalgic, Elegiac

Ah, the good old days. . . .

Brooks, Bill.
Pretty Boy. **2003.** Tor/Forge. 352pp. ISBN 0-765-30473-2.

> As the life of notorious outlaw Charley "Pretty Boy" Floyd ebbs—and flashes before him—in an Oklahoma field, the people who mattered to him, and some who merely crossed his path, comment on how his life has been led.

An elegiac picture of a man who embarked on his destiny even though it was obvious what its denouement would be.

Hickey, Elizabeth.
The Painted Kiss. **2005.** Atria. 256pp. ISBN 0-7434-9260-9.

Flash-forwards to the depths of World War II, when global disorder and destruction ruled the day, frame this elegiac, nostalgic story set in the twilight years of the Austro-Hungarian Empire and based on the lives of two historical figures: breakthrough artist Gustav Klimt and his much younger lover, Emilie Floge. Their relationship is not sensationalized, and the glitter of fin-de-siècle Vienna is palpable, as are the smell of paint in the artist's studio and his abject devotion to his art.

Jabotinsky, Vladimir.
The Fire: A Novel of Jewish Life in Turn-of-the-Century Odessa. **2005.** Cornell. 208pp. ISBN 0-80144266-4; paper. 208pp. ISBN 0-8014890-32.

The author, who died in 1940, was a controversial extremist-Zionist leader, yet his novel is a beautifully rendered, elegiac remembrance of and tribute to the Jewish community in the Russian city of Odessa when he was child, at the beginning of the twentieth century. The novel, written in 1935, was just recently published in English for the first time. It follows the fortunes of five siblings in an upper-middle-class Jewish family.

Morrison, Toni.
Love. **2003.** Knopf. 208pp. ISBN 0-375-40944-0; Vintage. paper. 202pp. ISBN 1-4000-7847-4.

In the 1940s and 1950s, powerful Bill Cosey ran a coastal hotel and resort popular with blacks for vacationing and enjoying food and dance. Now that Bill is dead, the women in his life struggle to exert their own kind of power in his absence. Exquisitely styled, as would be expected from the controlled but vastly creative pen of this Nobel laureate, this novel about personal relationships conjures the tone of a bygone time.

Turner, Frederick.
1929. **2003.** Counterpoint. 416pp. ISBN 1-58243-265-1.

America in the Roaring Twenties—specifically, the jazzy, illicit environment of the local speakeasy—is beautifully recalled in this fictional account of the life of Bix Beiderbecke, famous jazz coronet player. The short but swift life of this white musician is fondly remembered by the road manager of one of the bands with which Bix played. The tenor of the Jazz Age is caught here in all its brightness and syncopation.

Mysterious and Suspenseful

These novels conjure a deliciously ambiguous atmosphere that unsettles and intrigues readers.

Crowley, John.
Lord Byron's Novel. **2005.** Morrow. 352pp. ISBN 0-06-055658-7.

> The intriguing, absorbing premise of this novel is that it is possible that famous English poet Lord Byron left behind a novel manuscript, which his daughter assumed control of. A century-and-a-half later, with only a scrap of evidence of the manuscript's existence, an American researcher investigates whether the novel actually existed and what happened to it.

Fuentes, Carlos.
Old Gringo. **1985.** HarperCollins. paper. 199pp. ISBN 0-06-080938-8.

> In this relatively slender but trenchant and moving novel, the world-renowned contemporary Mexican novelist imagines the fate of early twentieth-century American writer Ambrose Bierce. Tradition has it that Bierce, who vanished in Mexico, did so when fighting with Pancho Villa's forces in the Mexican Revolution. Fuentes subscribes to that theory, not only reviving Bierce as a living, breathing individual but also imparting deeper dimensions to him through the reactions of a general in Villa's army and an American governess to him. Fuentes lets this beautifully concise narrative stand as an acute depiction of the clash of two cultures, American and Mexican.

Liss, David.
A Spectacle of Corruption. **2004.** Random. 400pp. ISBN 0-375-50855-4; Ballantine. paper. 416pp. ISBN 0-375-76089-X.

> The primary character, Benjamin Weaver, is a boxer turned private investigator, and the setting is eighteenth-century London. Weaver must prove himself innocent of a murder the courts want to hang him for. His pursuit takes him through all walks of society, and encounters corrupting forces throughout. Murder mystery, political thriller, and historical novel all in one, which here adds up to sheer excitement.

McGrath, Patrick.
Martha Peake: A Novel of the Revolution. **2000.** Random. 367pp. ISBN 0-375-50081-2; Vintage. paper. 367pp. ISBN 0-375-70131-1.

> The American Revolution is a common—but natural—time and place in which to set fiction, and this experienced author puts the inherent drama of that setting to good use. With gothic overtones, this novel is narrated by a young Englishman who visits his dying uncle, thinking he will inherit the old man's estate. The dying uncle relates to his nephew an elaborate tale about a deformed Cornish smuggler and his devoted daughter, whom, after he abuses

her, flees to America and becomes involved in the revolutionary movement; but just how reliable a narrator is the old man?

O'Connor, Joseph.
    Star of the Sea. **2002.** Harcourt. paper. 401pp. ISBN 0-15-602966-9.

        In the year 1847, Ireland is facing ruin from the potato famine and English misrule. A ship full of passengers in flight from their mistakes and setbacks sails for America's promise of a better future. But a murderer is also on board, and the spine-chilling, hair-raising drama never slackens.

Pearl, Matthew.
    The Dante Club. **2003.** Random. paper. 380pp. ISBN 0-8129-7104-3.

        Where the genres of murder mystery and historical novel meet—the hybrid subgenre of historical whodunits—is an appropriate way of defining this suspenseful, erudite, and quite articulate tale, set in Boston in 1865 and brimming with relevant social detail. It covers a series of murders, each related in some fashion to scenes in Dante's great masterpiece, *The Inferno.* The local Dante Club, whose members include such literary luminaries as Oliver Wendell Holmes and James Russell Lowell, must step in to solve the killings.

Scott, Sir Walter.
    The Heart of the Midlothian. 1818. Penguin. paper. 864pp. ISBN 0-14-043129-2.

        Considered by many of Scott's fans to be his best novel, this one is particularly rich in conjuring mystery and suspense *and* romance. The involved plot revolves around the efforts of a dairyman's daughter to save her sister from execution for child murder. But this basic plot line thickens and thickens as the novel develops, adding much to the novel's compelling nature and atmospheric texture.

Dark and Sinister Forces

It's a jungle out there, and these novels give clear proof of that fact.

Charyn, Jerome.
    The Green Lantern: A Romance of Stalinist Russia. **2004.** Thunder's Mouth. 368pp. ISBN 1-56858-312-5.

        The understandable paranoia in which people lived under the Stalinist dictatorship is palpable in this novel about the search for romance amid mad and evil times. Setting the narrative primarily in Moscow in the 1930s, Charyn finds two actors and their growing relationship the perfect objective correlative for depicting personal survival in the face of state-institutionalized terror.

Clarke, Clare.
The Great Stink. **2005.** Harcourt. 368pp. ISBN 0-15-101161-3.

It appears that Victorian London can never be exhausted as a rich, multilevel setting for historical fiction, and this first novel finds its own specific "arena," in the London sewer system! It seems that certain conditions in the British capital in 1855—excessive heat and a sewage overflow—combined to threaten to overwhelm the city; a cholera epidemic is at hand. An improvement in the city's infrastructure is obviously mandated, and into the picture—and into the political fray, as it turns out—steps engineer William May, a mentally fragile Crimean War veteran. Will he succumb to the civic corruption around him? Will he be freed from the asylum to which he has been consigned, as the major (but false) suspect in a murder (and will he continue to believe in his own innocence?) For fans of historical fiction with a good murder mystery woven into the fabric.

Finney, Paticia.
Firedrake's Eye. 1992. Picador. paper. 272pp. ISBN 0-312-18094-2.

Tudor England always lends itself well to dramatic, colorful historical fiction, and this thriller-like take on the times is exactly that: dramatic and colorful. Writing in a language appropriate to how people spoke and wrote in sixteenth-century England, Finney conjures a plot to assassinate Queen Elizabeth I by religious and political dissenters against her regime. The atmosphere of intrigue is compellingly evoked.

Franklin, Tom.
Hell at the Breech. 2003. Morrow. 320pp. ISBN 0-688-1674-1; Perennial. paper. 368pp. ISBN 0-06-056676-0.

Community versus community is the major thematic thread of this graphically violent but splendidly written novel set in Alabama in the 1890s. This very effective narrative is based on a real event: the murder of a local storekeeper running for political office and the resultant spree of revenge and vigilante justice that further polarized local landowners and the tenant farmers.

Martin, Valerie.
Property. 2003. Doubleday. 208pp. ISBN 0-385-50408-X; Vintage. paper. 193pp. ISBN 0-375-71330-1.

In 1828, on a Louisiana sugar plantation, Martin steadfastly, almost fiercely, investigates the impact of slavery on both black slaves and white owners as she develops a spellbinding, tension-filled tale of a white woman's obsessive loathing for her brutish husband and her simultaneous hatred for the black slave Sarah, her husband's reluctant mistress. All of this is set against the backdrop of a slave revolt, which brings to a head the white woman's intention of keeping Sarah as personal property.

Maxwell, Robin.
To the Tower Born. **2005.** Morrow. 320pp. ISBN 0-06-058051-8.

     Maxwell is an accomplished and popular revivifier of the Tudor era in English history; her admirable Elizabeth I quartet is composed of *The Secret Diary of Anne Boleyn* (1997), *The Queen's Bastard* (1999), *Virgin* (2001), and *The Wild Irish* (2003). In this novel, however, she sets aside the exciting and watershed Tudor period to peer into a more remote but no less exciting era of English history, when the House of York sat upon the highly contested throne. Maxwell obviously relishes her investigation—and offering her own well-considered interpretation—of one of the great mysteries of European history, the deaths of the boy-king Edward V and his little brother, the Duke of York, in the Tower of London, confined there by their usurping uncle, the infamous Richard III. The author's twist on events brings back the divisions at court that made these trying times for the country—but delicious reading for the contemporary lover of historical novels. You'll want to take sides yourself.

Reese, James.
The Book of Shadows. **2002.** Harper/Torch. paper. 623pp. ISBN 0-06-103184-4.

     The title of this first novel gives a rather clear indication of the dark, forbidding atmosphere that clings to every page of the story that follows. The first page further establishes the pervasive mood of the entire novel: "I vividly recall my mother's blood." OK! We're off and running in a gothic-tinged tale of witches and sorceries in post-revolutionary France. Herculine, the narrator, is an orphan living in a convent school; she has watched her mother bleed to death. She is released from the convent by a group of people who introduce her to a demonic, otherworldly world. She embarks on a physical journey across France and a "spiritual" one through the spirit world. For readers who enjoy a mix of historical novels and ghost stories.

Reese, James.
The Book of Spirits. **2005.** Morrow. 432pp. ISBN 0-06-056105-X.

     Where historical fiction and tales of the supernatural overlap is where Reese finds mesmerizing and even haunting common ground in a sequel to his atmospheric first novel, *The Book of Shadows* (above). The basic theme, initially presented in that book and expanded further here, is witchcraft, specifically that "practiced" in East Coast America in the early nineteenth century. And what a creative, graphic (as well as erotically charged) time Reese has with it—no easy task, since it a plot idea that has often been mined before. The hero-heroine (for he/she is a half-man, half-woman), Herculine, is borrowed from the previous novel (and now brought from France to the United States). Once in America, this riveting, carefully constructed character first channels her supernatural powers to aiding the slave community of Virginia. As the title indicates, the spiritual realm is where Herculine is at home—and writing about it is an obvious pleasure for the author.

Unsworth, Barry.
The Rage of the Vulture. **1982.** Norton. paper. 442pp. ISBN 0-393-31308-5.

The vulture of the title is Sultan Abdul Hamid II of Turkey, who, in 1908, the year in which the novel takes place, is more than just obsessed with maintaining his power—and his life—as the Ottoman Empire continues to crumble around him. All of this serves as a very colorful setting for an engaging story about a man in the British legation in Istanbul who is besieged by guilt for having witnessed the rape and murder of his American fiancée several years earlier.

Inspiring and Uplifting

These tales satisfy the need to believe that things can turn out for the best in good times and offer readers calm reassurance in troubled times.

Baldacci, David.
Wish You Well. **2000.** Warner. paper. 384pp. ISBN 0-446-61010-0.

Baldacci has secured a popular reputation for thrillers, but this time out he stepped into the historical fiction arena. The transfer from one genre to another caused him no misstep; this is an effective use of the historical past—the 1940s, to be exact. His "lack of experience" with the historical fiction genre does not impede his ability to conjure rural Virginia. Twelve-year-old Lou Cardinal and her younger brother, Oz, who live outside New York City, have lost their father in a car accident, and the incident has left their mother unable to respond anymore. They go to live with their great-grandmother, where they thrive on homemade food, riding horses, and plenty of sunshine. But then a coal company comes along that is interested in their great-grandmother's land. The novel's lesson is that the family that sticks together can defeat outside forces that don't have their best interests at heart.

Kennedy, William.
Ironweed. **1983.** Penguin. paper. 240pp. ISBN 0-14-007020-6.

Kennedy's highly regarded cycle of novels set in Albany, New York, in decades past includes this masterpiece, which won both the Pulitzer Prize and the National Book Critics Circle Awards. Along with *Roscoe*, it represents the high point of the author's illustrious series of novels. In 1938, Francis Phelan, ex-baseball player and now bum, has returned to Albany after an absence of 22 years. This is a lyrically styled novel, immaculately structured, about redemption and reconciliation. Kennedy usually focuses on down-and-out characters, insisting on seeing nobility in them.

Malamud, Bernard.

The Fixer. **1966.** Pocket. paper. 306pp. ISBN 0-6855-3965-2.

Malamud was one of the foremost American literary figures of the second half of the twentieth century. This Pulitzer Prize and National Book Award winner is a dark dissection of a moral dilemma, set in late Tsarist Russia. It concerns the anti-Semitism of that time, which results in unassuming Yakov Bak, a Jewish handyman, being falsely accused for the murder of a young boy, and the strength he generates by standing up to his accusers.

Tóibín, Colm.

The South. **1991.** Penguin. paper. 240pp. ISBN 0-14-014986-4.

With the careful attention to style that has since come to be the hallmark of this Irish writer, this first novel is about a thirty-something Irish woman who, in 1950, abandons home, Ireland, husband, and children to seek personal fulfillment in Franco's Spain. In the long term, the experiment fails, but not before the reader witnesses the woman's arrival at true maturity of spirit.

Urquhart, Jane.

The Stone Carvers. **2002.** Viking. 400pp. ISBN 0-670-0344-9; Penguin. paper. 400pp. ISBN 0-14-200358.

This highly regarded Canadian novelist offers a mesmerizing, imaginative, and stirring novel about a fictional brother-and sister team that carves a memorial to Canadian forces lost in World War I (there actually is such a monument near the French town of Arras). The author is simultaneously interested in the dynamic heritage of these two individuals, how they became stone carvers, and the separate trials and passions that have brought them and their talents together and restored their injured private lives. Clear, supple prose is what coalesces the novel into a stirring tale.

Wilder, Thornton.

The Bridge of San Luis Rey. **1927.** Perennial. paper. 160pp. ISBN 0-06-008887-7.

In 1714, the bridge of San Luis Rey, in colonial Peru, collapses, sending five people to their deaths below. The people who knew the victims learn from the tragedy an important lesson about the need for love and understanding. One of the great classics of American literature, this spare novel is timeless in its theme.

Humor

Believe it or not, a few historical novels are quite amusing and are to be read for comic enjoyment.

Heller, Joseph.
God Knows. **1984.** Simon & Schuster. paper. 368pp. ISBN 0-684-84125-8.

> Heller was one of the preeminent American novelists of the twentieth century, author of the classic antiwar novel *Catch-22*. His talent for comedy carried over into *God Knows*, which tells, in first-person narrative, the story of David, king of the Jews. This novel is something quite different than what the historical fiction reader usually encounters; its use of anachronisms is nothing short of brilliant, and the result is as hilarious as a good stand-up routine.

Holt, Thomas.
A Song for Nero. **2004.** Abacus. paper. 569pp. ISBN 0-349-11614-8.

> Humor abounds in this creative reinterpretation of the last days of the infamous Roman emperor Nero. History records that Nero killed himself as partisan forces headed in his direction with assassination in mind. But as Holt has it, these opposition forces actually killed Nero's look-alike, and the look-alike's brother and the not-at-all-dead emperor then experienced years of adventures in tandem.

Mosher, Howard Frank.
The True Account: A Novel of the Lewis and Clark and Kinneson Expeditions. **2003.** Mariner. paper. 338pp. ISBN 0-618-43123-3.

> The conceit of this marvelously inventive yarn is that a rival expedition force raced the Lewis and Clark group to the Pacific; in this take on history, one hilarious episode follows another, amounting to one big tall tale. The central character is Private True Teaque Kinneson, whose eccentric personality is given to both silliness and adventure. With his young nephew, Ticonderoga, he encounters great natural beauty but also unfriendly as well as friendly Indians, and the two must pass various tests. This is a Mark Twain-like take on the early nineteenth-century continental urge for exploration.

When the Fabric of the State Is Torn

Civil crises and disorder are always ripe for the historical novelist's plucking, and in the hands of good writers—which all the following are—the mood of civic and social unrest is made palpable.

Bernstein, Michael Andre.
Conspirators. **2004.** Farrar. 572pp. ISBN 0-314-23754-9.

This penetrating first novel is set in a corner of the Austro-Hungarian Empire just prior to the outbreak of World War I. The local provincial administrator must take measures to protect his region against civil unrest among the Jewish population, provoked by increasing anti-Semitism. Solidly researched and presented in considerable authoritative detail, this complex novel brings to light Jewish life in the declining years of the great Hapsburg dynasty.

De Bernières, Louis.
Birds without Wings. **2004.** Knopf. 554pp. ISBN 1-4000-4341-7.

From the author of the best-selling *Corelli's Mandolin* comes another compelling novel, this one focusing on a particular village in southwestern Anatolia. Its history, from the late nineteenth century to the early 1920s, is paradigmatic not only of the breakup of the Ottoman Empire but also of the atrocities and desperation that unfortunately accompanied the rise of the militant nationalism that defined the republican movement led by Mustafa Kemal. The author has the knack of bringing these large, overarching issues down to a personal level through a rich, varied cast of characters, each molded as a true individual and not simply a stock figure.

Dumas, Alexandre.
Queen Margot. **1845.** Hyperion. paper. 542pp. ISBN 0-786-88082-1.

Catholic princess Marguerite de Valois—"Margot"—was the sister of French king Charles IX. She married the Protestant king of Navarre, Henri de Bourbon. To read this richly detailed novel is to experience sixteenth-century France on an intimate basis during the deadly wars of persecution between Catholics and Protestants that nearly crippled the country. The fear with which people lived leaps from every page.

Dunnett, Dorothy.
The Game of Kings. **1961.** Vintage. paper. 560pp. ISBN 0-679-77743-1.

Dunnet is one of the most highly regarded contemporary historical novelists, and one of her most popular cycles of novels is her six-part Lymond Chronicles, of which *The Game of Kings* is the first installment. The time is 1547, and Scotland not only faces invasion by its southern neighbor but also suffers from internecine struggles among its nobles. The hero of the hour is Francis Crawford of Lymond, whose flamboyance provides sheer entertainment.

Gregory, Philippa.
Earthly Joys. **1998.** Touchstone. paper. 528pp. ISBN 0-7432-7252-8.

The best-selling author of *That Other Boleyn Girl*, *The Virgin's Lover*, and *The Queen's Fool* continues her exciting reconstruction of the momentous Tudor era in English history, this time moving her storyline along to the

Stuart succession to the great Elizabeth I and bringing telling light to the political and religious tumult and chaos of pre-Restoration England. The focus is gardener John Tradescent, working for the seductive Duke of Buckingham, and through John's experiences the reader is shown a wide and detailed picture of the effects on personal life of Stuart absolutism and the increasing disdain of the Parliament for the increasingly inflexible monarchy.

Pushkin, Alexander.
The Captain's Daughter. **1836.** Vintage. paper. 320pp. ISBN 0-394-70714-1.

Pushkin, a major figure in Russian literature, painted in controlled prose the portraits of a group of lively characters in this absorbing novel, which he set in his native land in the late eighteenth century. It is based on a real incident: the uprising of a Cossack group, led by a man claiming to be the recently deceased czar, Peter III. In the midst of this a poignant love story is played out.

Sienkiewicz, Henryk.
Quo Vadis. **1895.** Hippocrene. paper. 589pp. ISBN 0-78108550-3.

The Roman Empire in the first century after the birth of Christ springs to life in this extremely dramatic novel centered on a young Roman patrician, Vinicius, and his obsession with a beautiful young Christian woman, daughter of a foreign king, who does not live in Rome. Vinicius converts to Christianity, and the drama of the novel is spun from the heightened atmosphere—so well conjured here—of political intrigue at the highest levels and the persecution of Christians and anyone else at odds with Emperor Nero.

Smith, Wilbur.
River God. **1994.** St. Martin's. paper. 664pp. ISBN 0-312-95446-8.

This absorbing novel, brimming with a wealth of abundant (but consistently relevant) detail about the customs of the country, ushers the reader into a provocative period of the past, for the reader almost as if in an actual time machine because of the real sense of being there it imparts. Accomplished and popular historical novelist Smith chooses a period in the history of ancient Egypt when the pharaonic line had descended into weakness, foreign enemies were waiting at the gates, and the Upper and Lower Kingdoms threatened to tear asunder, but it was also a time of great heroic deeds.

Vidal, Gore.
Julian. **1964.** Vintage. paper. 528pp. ISBN 0-375-72706-X.

The contemporary American master of the literary historical novel reached back with great authority, to say nothing of his trademark eloquence and nimbleness of style, to ancient times and came up with this delightful, amusing, intelligent treatment of the nature and corrosiveness of power at a time of intense religious upheaval. Roman emperor Julian has spent time and energy attempting to restore the old pantheon of gods in the face of the rising appeal of Christianity. It is now A.D. 30 A.D.; Julian is deceased, and Emperor Theodosius of the Eastern Roman Empire has not only converted to Christianity but also has made his new faith mandatory for everyone within the Eastern realm. Julian's teacher combines a fragment of the late ruler's memoir with his own sympathetic reconstruction of Julian's life story, to "show the justice of his contest with the Christians." A heady and exciting novel.

Spies Among Us

In these riveting novels, people are watching, and telling other people what they see. Intrigue and suspicion permeate these stories.

Falconer, Colin.
The Sultan's Harem. **2004.** Crown. 480pp. ISBN 0-609-61030-9.

Inherent in stories about the Ottoman Empire is a mood of intrigue and court duplicity. Readers looking for that mood won't be disappointed by this riveting novel, based on the sixteenth-century sultan Suleyman the Magnificent and his besottedness with one of his concubines, who is hell-bent on revenge for her enslavement at the spy-riddled court.

Finney, Patricia.
Gloriana's Torch. **2003.** St. Martin's. 464pp. ISBN 0-312-31285-7.

This is the last installment in the author's trilogy (all three titles can stand separately) about the court of the great Tudor queen, Elizabeth I (see also *Firedrake's Eye* and *Unicorn's Blood*). Finney maintains the thriller atmosphere she so effectively conjured in the previous novels. The Spanish are preparing their armada against England and a large amount of gunpowder has gone missing from the queen's reserves. Is there a traitor in the English midst?

France, John.
Lucrezia Borgia. **2003.** Three Rivers. 282pp. ISBN 1-4000-5122-3.

This author's first novel captures the atmosphere of decadence and deceit at the Vatican court of Pope Alexander VI—born Rodrigo Borgia, and father of the notorious Lucrezia, here depicted as an intelligent woman desiring to realize her own life choices despite her father's use of her to further his political ambitions.

Furst, Alan.
The World at Night. **1996.** Random. paper. 268pp. ISBN 0-375-75858-5.
Red Gold. **1999.** Random. paper. 266pp. ISBN 0-375-75859-3.

Are the absolutely addicting novels of Furst historical thrillers or spy thrillers? His growing number of avid readers would shrug their shoulders, not out of perplexity but out of indifference to the question. These two novels, the latter a sequel to the former, feature French film producer Jean Casson, who must face the very personal consequences of the German occupation in 1940. Furst's novels, set all across Europe, are at once lusciously and starkly evocative of the life-and-death atmosphere of the periods prior to and during World War II.

Warp and Weave

These novels are about the way society is composed, the fabric from which customs are constructed. They paint concrete pictures of the atmosphere of the particular society in which each takes place.

Byatt, A. S.
A Whistling Woman. **2002.** Vintage. paper. 448pp. ISBN 0-679-77690-7.

As is the case with its immediate predecessor in Byatt's quartet of novels about English provincial and city life in the 1950s and 1960s, Babel Tower, the fourth and final installment features the deeply layered character Frederica, who has traveled from country life to London, from being a young intellectual to a mature woman involved in the television industry. As in all three of the previous novels in the quartet (the first two being *The Virgin in the Garden* and *Still Life*), Byatt's characters are the probes with which she elaborately explores how those watershed years in English culture affected a variety of individuals and personalities.

Cather, Willa.
Shadows on the Rock. **1931.** Penguin. paper. 240pp. ISBN 0-679-76404-6.

This eminent American novelist's keen knowledge of the customs of seventeenth-century colonial Quebec results in a vivid, warm, deeply human novel composed of beautifully rendered set pieces—which, however, coalesce into a strong and powerfully integrated narrative. The teenager Cecile gives great support to her apothecary father during the winter months when New France is essentially shut in from the world, shut off from the mother country, France.

Ceely, Jonathan.
Mina. **2004.** Delta. paper. 336pp. ISBN 0-385-33688-8.

In the nineteenth century, an Irish girl escaping her sad childhood is employed as a servant in the kitchen of an English estate, disguised as a boy. She eventually confesses her true identity and her Irish past to the estate's cook; he in turn shares his secrets. A friendship grows amid the author's luxurious descriptions of Victorian life, especially food preparation.

Dunant, Susan.

The Birth of Venus. **2004.** Random. 400pp. ISBN 1-4000-6073-7.

Set in Renaissance (fifteenth-century) Florence and Italy, Dunant's compelling novel (she is a veteran thriller writer, and obviously from that experience she is knowledgeable about how to construct a suspenseful narrative) centers on a teenage girl's fascination with art and an influential artist, as religious persecution consigns sophisticated and cultured Florence to a streak of fundamentalism.

Eliot, George.

Romola. **1863.** Penguin. paper. 688pp. ISBN 0-14043470-4.

From one of the absolute giants of English literature comes this novel set in fifteenth-century Florence, with a plot that is not easy to follow. It centers on the less-than-noble adventurer Tito and his pursuit of the sweet Romola, daughter of a Florentine scholar. The major and minor characters are all deeply layered and, importantly, the author imbues the times with rich color.

Garrett, George.

The Succession: A Novel of Elizabeth and James. **1983.** Harvest. paper. 552pp. ISBN 0-15-686303-0.

Entered from the Sun: The Murder of Marlowe. **1990.** Harvest. paper. 372pp. ISBN 0-15-628795-1.

The first volume in Garrett's riveting trilogy about Elizabethan England, *Death of the Fox* (1971), has gone out of print; it focused on the life of Sir Walter Raleigh. The trilogy's second and third volumes fortunately remain in print. The second installment, *The Succession*, reconstructs the concluding years of the reign of Elizabeth I, as James VI of Scotland waits to replace her on the English throne. The third part of the trilogy, *Entered from the Sun*, involves a pair of men, in the employ of opposing factions, investigating the stabbing death of poet-playwright Christopher Marlowe. Their charge is to determine the surrounding circumstances: Was it a more-or-less innocent drunken brawl, or a political assassination? The trilogy is outstanding in re-creating the tense atmosphere of the times, accomplished with concrete details and a fluid writing style.

Hicks, Robert.

The Widow of the South. **2005.** Warner. 409pp. ISBN 0-446-50012-7.

An emotionally gripping novel based on the life of an actual person by the name of Carrie McGavock, who in 1864 witnessed the Battle of Franklin, Tennessee, which took place virtually at her doorstep. At a later point, she and her husband reburied the bodies of 1,000 Confederate dead in a plot of their own land and thus owned the only private Confederate cemetery. The battle itself, the preparations on both sides leading up to it, and the short-term and long-term physical and psychological consequences of it on both observers and participants are rendered in sharp, eloquent prose, told from the perspectives of both Carrie and her husband, Union and Confederate soldiers, and others. A very vivid look at what war does and how people finally accommodate themselves to its destruction.

Scott, Manda.
    Dreaming the Eagle. **2003.** Delacorte. 480pp. ISBN 0-385-33670-5; Delta. paper. 480pp. ISBN 0-385-33773-6.
    Dreaming the Bull. **2004.** Delacorte. 368pp. ISBN 0-385-33671-3.

        A planned quartet, of which these are the first two volumes, follows the life of Boudica, the first-century A.D Celtic noble girl who ultimately successfully led troops into battle against the Romans. These companion novels define "sweeping epic," limning the tribal culture of pre-Roman Britain and what the advent of the Romans meant to the survival of Celtic culture.

Settle, Mary Lee.
    The Scapegoat. **1980.** University of South Carolina. paper. 278pp. ISBN 1-57003-117-7.

        The fourth installment in Settle's impressive Beulah Quintet follows *Know Nothing* and brings the story of the Virginia families whose destinies the author has been tracing up to the post–Civil War era, when organized labor and unionization swept the coal mines that were the life and sustenance of West Virginia. As in the previous novels in the sequence, Settle is excellent at capturing the dress of the time and how clothes bespoke class differentiation.

Encountering Prejudice

Prejudice comes not exclusively in the form of racism.

Barker, Pat.
    The Eye in the Door. **1994.** Plume. paper. 288pp. ISBN 0-452-27272-6.

        In this sequel to the author's psychologically incisive *Regeneration*, further consequences of the effects of the horrible trench warfare of 1914–1918 on the home front in Britain are explored—namely, the persecution of pacifists and the witch hunt for "deviants" (homosexuals, that is). This novel accurately and searingly reflects the inner tensions of that earth- , body- , and soul-shattering time.

Barry, Sebastian.
    A Long Long Way. **2005.** Viking. 288pp. ISBN 0-670-03380-4.

        This Irish novelist and playwright sets his powerful and dark novel during World War I. Young Willie Dunne enlists to fight the Germans, and the battle scenes are realistically, even gruesomely, drawn, but behind what takes place on the battlefield are the great tensions between the Irish and their English landlords back home.

Bradley, John Ed.
Restoration. **2003.** Anchor. paper. 320pp. ISBN 0-385-72116-1.

When discussing historical novels, the term "restoration" is usually associated with the return of the Stuart monarchy to England and Scotland after the Cromwell-Puritan interregnum of the mid-seventeenth century. But in this thoughtful novel, the word refers to racial divides in the New Orleans of the early 1940s. Recently retired but still in his thirties, fed-up journalist Jack Charbonnet gets involved with black art conservator Rhys Goudean and thus involved in her pursuit of the mysterious life and death of a promising young artist forced to destroy a work depicting interracial dancing. Their inquiry takes them back to the racial and artistic past of the Big Easy as well as forcing them to confront still-existing attitudes about race.

Holdstock, Pauline.
A Rare and Curious Gift. **2005.** Norton. 352pp. ISBN 0-393-05968-5.

Medieval Florence naturally provides a colorful, nearly tactile setting for a drama involving art and the artist's life. In this case, Sofonisba, daughter of an artist, although a brilliant painter, is downgraded or overlooked because of her gender. Holdstock bases her on the real-life Artemisia Gentileschi, drawing on events from that woman's life to authenticate her portrait of Florentine painters and, especially, women artists. Sofonisba's passion extends to her sexual nature, adding to the novel's verisimilitude.

Morrison, Toni.
Jazz. **1992.** Vintage. paper. 256pp. ISBN 1-4000-7621-8.

Three of this Nobel laureate's magnificent novels can be considered historical: *Beloved, Love,* and this one. Morrison uses history in her fiction to go deeply into her characters (who are her own invention, not actual personages) to find within their psyches the specific social and economic forces that oppress or sustain black freedom on an individual, personal level. *Jazz* takes place in the Harlem of the 1920s, telling the love story of now-middle-aged Joe Trace, a women's beauty-products salesman, and his wife, Violet, to whom he has been married for two decades. In its specific focus, it reveals the effects of his just having shot his teenage lover. This sensuous, sobering story of love and obsession carried out amid and stamped by racial sentiments of the time, is delivered in Morrison's syncopated prose style, so appropriate to the milieu.

Stevenson, Jane.

The Shadow King. **2003.** Houghton. 303pp. ISBN 0-618-14913-9; Mariner. paper. 320pp. ISBN 0-618-48536-8.

This sequel to the author's *Winter Queen* extends the story of Elizabeth Stuart, sister of England's early-seventeenth-century king (beheaded during the English Civil War) Charles I. She was dubbed the "Winter Queen" of Bohemia, and her apparent, speculative, secret husband was an ex-slave and African prince. But the focus of this novel is their son, Baltasar Stuart, a physician who, from Holland to London to the Barbados, must cope with his anomalous status: black or white, royal or commoner? An inventive novel.

Vreeland, Susan.

The Passion of Artemesia. **2002.** Penguin. paper. 352pp. ISBN 0-14-200182-1.

As she did in the compelling *Girl in Hyacinth Blue*, Vreeland captures the psychological and emotional textures of life as affected by art. Her focus is a historical figure, seventeenth-century Italian female painter Artemisia Gentileschi, who here emerges as a sort of proto-feminist, struggling to handle domestic occupations and a career in a field hugely dominated by men, as well as to find the recognition as an artist that she desires.

Index

About the Author

BRAD HOOPER is the Adult Books Editor at *Booklist* magazine, the review journal for public and school libraries published by the American Library Association. Historical fiction is a particular interest and specialty of his. Brad holds the MSLS degree and worked as a reference librarian in the History Department of the Cleveland Public Library before going to *Booklist*. In his capacity as Adult Books Editor, he is a frequent panelist and speaker at library and publisher meetings and has given many book-review-writing workshops to public librarians across the country.

He is the author of *The Fiction of Ellen Gilchrist: An Appreciation* and *The Short Story Readers' Advisory: A Guide to the Best*.